Bark-Worthy Bites

Chef-Quality Treats for Your Four-Legged Foodie, Quick, Health-Boosting Recipes for Busy Pet Owners Who Want the Best for Their Dogs

Lucy Irving

© **Copyright 2024 - All rights reserved.**

The content contained within this book may not be reproduced, duplicated or transmitted without direct written permission from the author or the publisher.

Under no circumstances will any blame or legal responsibility be held against the publisher, or author, for any damages, reparation, or monetary loss due to the information contained within this book. Either directly or indirectly.

Lucy Irving

Legal Notice:

This book is copyright protected. This book is only for personal use. You cannot amend, distribute, sell, use, quote or paraphrase any part, or the content within this book, without the consent of the author or publisher.

Disclaimer Notice:

Please note the information contained within this document is for educational and entertainment purposes only. All effort has been executed to present accurate, up to date, and reliable, complete information. No warranties of any kind are declared or implied. Readers acknowledge that the author is not engaging in the rendering of legal, financial, medical or professional advice. The content within this book has been derived from various sources. Please consult a licensed professional before attempting any techniques outlined in this book.

By reading this document, the reader agrees that under no circumstances is the author responsible for any losses, direct or indirect, which are incurred as a result of the use of information contained within this document, including, but not limited to, — errors, omissions, or inaccuracies.

TABLE OF CONTENTS

Introduction 9
    Understanding your dog's nutritional needs: 9
    The benefits of homemade dog treats: 9
    Navigating dog food allergies and sensitivities: 10
    Safety and storage 10
    Building community 11

Chapter 1: Setting Up Your Dog Treat Kitchen 12
    Essential Equipment and Ingredients 13
    Safety Guidelines and Foods to Avoid 13
    Organizing Your Cooking Space 14

Chapter 2: Dog Nutrition 101 16
    The Basics of a Balanced Dog Diet 17
    Understanding Ingredients: What to Use and Why 18
    Supplements: Are They Necessary? 19

Chapter 3: Simple and Basic Treats 21
    1. Peanut Butter Pup cakes 21
    2. Carrot and Oat Dog Biscuits 22
    3. Cheesy Sweet Potato Chews 23
    4. Banana and Blueberry Frozen Treats 24
    5. Chicken and Brown Rice Balls 25
    6. Pumpkin and Cinnamon Cookies 26
    7. Salmon and Sweet Potato Sticks 27
    8. Spinach and Cheese Bites 28
    9. Turkey and Cranberry Jerky 29
    10. Apple and Cheddar Pup cakes 30
    11. Beef and Potato Bites 31

12. Cranberry and Pumpkin Doggy Donuts 32

13. Turkey Bacon Bites 33

14. Blueberry and Banana Muffins 34

15. Cheese and Bacon Twists 35

16. Peanut Butter and Banana Frozen Treats 36

17. Liver and Carrot Bites 37

18. Pumpkin and Peanut Butter Biscuits 38

19. Turkey and Veggie Meatballs 39

20. Apple and Carrot Crunchies 40

21. Spinach and Salmon Bites 41

22. Pumpkin and Carrot Pup cakes 42

23. Turkey and Rice Cookies 43

24. Sweet Potato and Banana Treats 44

25. Chicken and Pumpkin Poppers 45

26. Blueberry and Coconut Cookies 46

27. Liver and Oatmeal Biscuits 47

28. Turkey and Cranberry Poppers 48

29. Carrot and Peanut Butter Cookies 49

30. Banana and Peanut Butter Frozen Pops 50

31. Apple and Cheddar Biscuits 51

32. Peanut Butter and Jelly Bites 52

33. Turkey and Vegetable Patties 53

34. Blueberry and Banana Pup Pops 54

35. Chicken and Spinach Balls 55

36. Carrot and Zucchini Chips 56

37. Salmon and Sweet Potato Balls 57

38. Banana and Carrot Biscotti 58

39. Turkey and Quinoa Balls 59

40. Pumpkin and Cinnamon Twists 60

41. Cheese and Parsley Biscuits 61

42. Pumpkin and Peanut Butter Bites 62

43. Chicken and Carrot Cookies 63

44. Blueberry and Banana Twists 64

45. Turkey and Cranberry Cookies 65

46. Spinach and Feta Bites 66

47. Carrot and Apple Chips 67

48. Turkey and Sweet Potato Muffins 68

49. Chicken and Cheese Balls 69

50. Blueberry and Carrot Muffins 70

Introduction to Easy Recipes 71

    Single-Ingredient Wonders 72

    Basic Biscuits and Chews 73

Chapter 4: Special Dietary Needs 75

    Grain-Free Treats 76

    Low-Calorie Snacks 77

    Hypoallergenic Options 78

Chapter 5: Training Treats and Rewards 79

    High-Value Motivators 80

    Small Bites for Frequent Rewards 81

    Chicken and Sweet Potato Squares: 81

    Peanut Butter and Banana Balls: 82

    Cheesy Oatmeal Bites: 83

    Long-lasting chews for Extended Engagement 84

    Sweet Potato Chews: 84

    Frozen Carrot Sticks: 85

    Peanut Butter Stuffed Kong: 86

Chapter 6: Seasonal and Celebration Treats 87

    Festive Holiday Snacks 88

Christmas Turkey Bites: 88

Easter Carrot Pup cakes: 89

Halloween Pumpkin Treats: 90

Thanksgiving Cranberry Cookies: 91

Valentine's Day Berry Hearts: 92

Birthday and Party Treats 93

Peanut Butter Pup cakes: 93

Cheesy Bone Biscuits: 94

Apple and Carrot Paws: 95

Blueberry Banana Bites: 96

Salmon and Sweet Potato Stars: 97

Cooling Summer Snacks 98

Frozen Yogurt Drops: 98

Watermelon Ice Cubes: 99

Cucumber Mint Bites: 100

Coconut Water Popsicles: 101

Frozen Blueberry Bites: 102

Chapter 7: Advanced Nutritious Recipes 103

Superfood Snacks 104

Homemade Meals and Meal Toppers 105

Therapeutic Treats for Health Issues 106

Chapter 8: Storing and Preserving Your Homemade Treats 108

Safe Storage Practices 109

Freezing and Dehydrating 110

Best Before: Understanding Shelf Life 111

Shopping list of all ingredients used in the recipes. 113

Conclusion: 120

Reiterating the Joy and Benefits of Homemade Dog Treats 120

Encouraging Continuous Learning and Experimentation 121

Building a Community of Health-Conscious Dog Owners.. 122
Recipe Development and Writing Style Notes: 122

"Welcome to your journey into homemade dog treats! As we embark on this path together, I would be deeply grateful if you could consider leaving a review on Amazon after you've explored the recipes. Your feedback not only means a lot to me personally, given the hard work and love poured into this book, but it also assists in spreading the word to other dog lovers about the benefits of nutritious, homemade treats. Thank you in advance for your kindness and support—it truly helps!"

Introduction

Welcome to Healthy Homemade Dog Treats, where love meets nutrition for your beloved companions. Our recipes are carefully crafted using simple ingredients and easy instructions. Each treat is designed to prioritize your dog's health, free of additives, and full of flavor. We celebrate originality by offering different recipes tailored to each puppy's unique taste. With affordable ingredients and no need for special equipment, preparing these treats is a breeze. Explore our selection, tailored to various dietary needs, and find the perfect snack for your furry friend. Prioritize their well-being by checking the nutritional information provided. Embark on a journey of culinary joy that nourishes the body and soul.

Understanding your dog's nutritional needs:

Understanding your dog's nutritional needs is critical to their well-being. Just like us, they require a balanced diet rich in protein, fat, carbohydrates, vitamins, and minerals. High-quality proteins, such as lean meats and fish, support muscle development and repair. Essential fatty acids from sources such as salmon maintain healthy skin and brain function, while carbohydrates from whole grains and vegetables provide energy and aid digestion. When preparing homemade delicacies, choose natural and healthy ingredients over artificial additives. By prioritizing a balanced diet, you can ensure that your dog has a happy and healthy life. Every dog has unique dietary needs and preferences that vary by age, breed, health status, and activity level. Younger dogs may require high-protein, high-energy treats to support their growth and boundless energy, while older dogs may benefit from ingredients that support joint health and cognitive function. Dogs with health issues such as allergies, obesity, or digestive problems may particularly benefit from homemade treats tailored to directly address these concerns. This book offers a myriad of recipes designed to meet these.

The benefits of homemade dog treats:

Homemade dog treats offer unparalleled benefits, promoting health and strengthening bonds. Unlike store-bought options, homemade treats allow precise control over ingredients, ensuring a healthy diet free of harmful additives. Customizing recipes to address dietary issues such as allergies or sensitivities promotes both safety and enjoyment for our furry friends.

Beyond nutrition, creating treats at home nurtures the relationship between pet and owner. Sharing moments in the kitchen improves trust and communication as dogs eagerly await the rewards of shared experiences. The variety of ingredients in homemade treats ensures a balanced diet and prevents food monotony, promoting healthy eating habits.

In addition, homemade treats serve as powerful training aids, reinforcing positive behaviors and nurturing obedience. By investing in homemade treats, owners invest in the well-being and happiness of their beloved companions, enriching their lives with love, care, and attention.

Navigating dog food allergies and sensitivities:

Understanding and managing food allergies and sensitivities in dogs is critical to their health. Similar to humans, dogs can also experience negative reactions to specific foods, causing discomfort and health problems. Identifying common allergens and making informed dietary choices can alleviate symptoms and improve their quality of life.

A common allergy in dogs is celiac disease, or gluten intolerance. Gluten, found in grains such as wheat, barley, and rye, can trigger reactions such as gastrointestinal upset and skin irritation. Opting for grain-free or gluten-free ingredients such as coconut flour or almond meal is essential for dogs with gluten intolerance.

Protein sensitivity is also common. Ingredients such as beef, chicken, and dairy can cause digestive problems or rashes. Consider alternative proteins such as turkey and fish and plant-based options such as lentils. Monitor your dog's response to ingredients and consult your veterinarian if you suspect allergies.

Being proactive in identifying and managing food allergies improves your dog's well-being. Choose ingredients carefully for homemade treats, avoiding common allergens. Prioritize your dog's health by selecting ingredients that support his unique needs.

Safety and storage

Knowing how to safely prepare and store homemade dog treats is critical. This guide not only provides recipes; it also teaches you how to make sure treats are cooked properly to avoid pathogens and how to store them safely to maintain freshness and prevent spoilage. You'll learn everything from the basics of dog food safety to advanced tips for long-term storage.

Building community

Finally, this journey is not one you embark on alone. In this book, we encourage you to connect with a community of like-minded pet owners who are embracing the homemade approach. Sharing experiences and recipes, discussing what works and what doesn't, and supporting each other in pet health challenges can make the process of creating homemade treats even more rewarding.

As we delve into the following chapters, remember that each recipe is a starting point. Experimentation and customization are encouraged to perfect these treats for your special friend's palate and dietary needs. So preheat the oven, gather the ingredients, and get ready to transform the way you think about dog treats. Let's make every snack a step toward better health and more joyful times together!

Chapter 1: Setting Up Your Dog Treat Kitchen

Embarking on the journey of creating homemade dog treats is not only rewarding but also begins with setting up a well-equipped kitchen. This ensures a seamless treat-making process and allows for the creation of delightful snacks for your furry companion.

Start by establishing a clean and organized workspace dedicated solely to making dog treats. Designate a specific area in your kitchen where ingredients can be safely prepared and stored, minimizing the risk of cross-contamination with human food. Keep countertops and utensils sanitized to uphold food safety standards.

Gather essential kitchen tools and equipment, though specialized appliances aren't necessary. Basic items such as mixing bowls, measuring cups and spoons, a rolling pin, various cookie cutters, baking sheets, and parchment paper can enhance efficiency and consistency in the preparation process.

Since we are dealing with ingredients, simplicity is fundamental. Stock your pantry with dog-friendly options like whole wheat flour, oats, peanut butter (ensuring it's xylitol-free), unsweetened applesauce, pumpkin puree, bananas, eggs, and lean proteins such as chicken or turkey. Opt for high-quality, natural ingredients devoid of artificial additives, preservatives, and sugars.

For dogs with dietary concerns, consider alternative ingredients such as gluten-free flour, hypoallergenic protein sources like salmon or duck, and natural sweeteners such as honey or molasses. Maintaining a variety of ingredients allows for recipe adaptation based on your dog's needs.

Invest in proper storage containers to keep homemade treats fresh. Once the treats have cooled after being baked in the oven, they can be stored at room temperature or in the refrigerator by placing them in airtight containers or resealable bags, as the recipe suggests. Label containers with treat names and preparation dates for freshness tracking.

With the right setup of tools, ingredients, and storage solutions, your dog treat kitchen will be primed for a culinary adventure that both you and your furry friend will relish. Let creativity and love guide you as you create homemade treats that nourish your dog's body and soul.

Essential Equipment and Ingredients

Crafting nutritious homemade dog treats requires only basic equipment and a handful of simple, wholesome ingredients tailored to your furry friend's palate and needs. Equipping yourself with the right tools and ingredients empowers you to effortlessly whip up delectable treats that align with your dog's dietary requirements and preferences.

You don't need fancy gadgets; standard kitchen tools suffice, making homemade treat preparation accessible to all pet owners. Essential items like mixing bowls, measuring cups and spoons, a rolling pin, cookie cutters, baking sheets, and parchment paper streamline the mixing, shaping, and baking processes, ensuring consistent results.

Simplicity is key when it comes to ingredients. Choose natural, whole-food options safe for dogs, such as whole wheat flour, oats, xylitol-free peanut butter, unsweetened applesauce, pumpkin puree, bananas, eggs, and lean proteins like chicken or turkey. These ingredients provide a balanced mix of nutrients to support your dog's overall health.-

To accommodate dietary concerns, consider alternatives like gluten-free flour, hypoallergenic proteins such as salmon or duck, and natural sweeteners like honey or molasses. Customizing recipes with these options ensures your treats suit your dog's specific needs while remaining nutritious and delicious.

Prioritize quality and freshness in ingredient selection, opting for items free from artificial additives, preservatives, and added sugars. Choose organic or locally sourced ingredients when possible to maximize nutritional value.

Ensure you use appropriate containers to keep the treats fresh. Airtight containers or resealable bags work best for storing them at room temperature or in the fridge. To monitor their freshness, label the containers with the treat names and the dates they were made.

With your kitchen stocked with essential tools and ingredients, you're ready for a homemade dog treat-making adventure. Let your creativity and love shine through as you create treats that not only delight your dog's taste buds but also contribute to their overall well-being and happiness.

Safety Guidelines and Foods to Avoid

Ensuring the safety and well-being of our furry friends is paramount when preparing healthy homemade dog treats. Following specific guidelines and being mindful of potentially harmful ingredients is essential to crafting treats that are both nutritious and safe for your pet.

Begin by carefully examining the list of ingredients for any possible allergens or harmful substances. Foods like chocolate, onions, garlic, grapes, raisins, macadamia nuts, and xylitol are known to be harmful to dogs, even in small amounts. Avoid these ingredients altogether to prevent adverse reactions ranging from gastrointestinal upset to severe symptoms like seizures or organ failure.

Furthermore, be wary of ingredients that could cause choking or digestive problems. Cooked bones might splinter and inflict internal damage, while big chunks of rawhide or other non-digestible chews could present choking risks. Opt for safe alternatives like finely ground oats or shredded carrots, ensuring treats are easy for dogs to chew and digest.

Mindful preparation extends to avoiding cross-contamination in a shared kitchen. Use separate utensils, cutting boards, and equipment to prevent contact with harmful substances or allergens. Carefully wash and disinfect all surfaces and tools both before and after making treats to reduce the chance of contamination.

When baking treats, maintain accurate oven temperatures and cooking times to avoid undercooking or burning. Use oven thermometers to verify settings and closely monitor treats while baking for the desired texture and doneness.

By adhering to these safety guidelines and mindful practices, you can create homemade dog treats that are both delicious and safe. By choosing ingredients meticulously and using proper preparation methods, you can offer your pet wholesome snacks that enhance their overall well-being and joy.

Organizing Your Cooking Space

Creating healthy homemade dog treats is a delightful endeavor that thrives in an organized and efficient cooking space. By optimizing your kitchen setup and streamlining your workflow, you can elevate your cooking experience and effortlessly whip up delectable treats for your furry friend.

Begin by decluttering and cleaning your kitchen to foster a welcoming cooking environment. Clear countertops of unnecessary items and arrange cabinets and drawers for easy access to essential tools and ingredients. A tidy kitchen not only boosts efficiency but also enhances the joy of cooking and baking.

Designate a specific area solely for preparing dog treats, distinct from spaces used for human food. This separation prevents cross-contamination, ensuring treats remain safe and hygienic. Set up a dedicated workspace with a clean surface where you can comfortably mix ingredients, roll out dough, and shape treats.

Invest in storage solutions to keep ingredients organized and accessible. Use clear containers or labeled jars for dry ingredients like flour and oats, and store perishables in designated areas to maintain freshness.

Arrange cooking utensils and tools for effortless access. Keep frequently used items like mixing bowls, measuring cups, spatulas, and baking sheets nearby. Consider installing hooks or racks on walls to hang utensils, keeping them organized and visible.

Maximize efficiency by planning and gathering all ingredients and equipment before starting. Review recipes ahead of time and create a checklist to ensure everything is on hand. Pre-measure ingredients and set them out in individual containers to streamline cooking and minimize the risk of overlooking an item.

Maintain a tidy space throughout the baking process by cleaning up as you go. Wash dishes, utensils, and countertops promptly to prevent clutter buildup and simplify cleanup once treats are in the oven.

With an organized and tidy cooking space, you can enjoy stress-free baking experiences while creating delicious homemade treats for your cherished canine companion.

Chapter 2: Dog Nutrition 101

Mastering the fundamentals of dog nutrition is key to crafting a diet that nurtures your furry companion's well-being. By grasping their nutritional requirements and choosing fitting ingredients for homemade treats, you ensure they receive the vital nutrients needed for a thriving life.

Proteins stand as the foundation of a dog's diet, vital for maintaining robust muscles, tissues, and organs. Opt for top-notch protein sources like lean meats (such as chicken, turkey, and beef), fish, eggs, and dairy in homemade treats to furnish your dog with essential amino acids, bolstering their overall health.

Fats constitute another pivotal element in a dog's diet, furnishing concentrated energy and essential fatty acids. Incorporate omega-3 and omega-6 fatty acids from sources like salmon, flaxseed, and chicken fat into homemade treats to promote lustrous skin, a glossy coat, and optimal brain function while combating inflammation.

Carbohydrates serve to fuel dogs' energy reserves and provide essential fiber, fostering digestion and a sense of satiety. Although carnivorous by nature, dogs can benefit from wholesome carbohydrates derived from whole grains, fruits, and vegetables. Opt for complex carbohydrates such as brown rice, sweet potatoes, and carrots in homemade treats to ensure sustained energy levels without causing undesirable blood sugar spikes.

Vitamins and minerals are indispensable for upholding overall health in dogs. Incorporate a diverse array of fruits and vegetables into homemade treats to supply your furry friend with essential vitamins, minerals, and antioxidants. Blueberries, pumpkin, spinach, and carrots are stellar choices, fortifying your dog's immune system and vitality.

When whipping up homemade treats, steer clear of ingredients potentially harmful to dogs, such as chocolate, onions, garlic, grapes, raisins, and artificial sweeteners like xylitol. These substances can trigger adverse reactions, from digestive issues to severe conditions like kidney failure or neurological complications. Always check labels and choose safe and suitable ingredients for canine consumption.

By embracing the basics of dog nutrition and selecting nourishing ingredients for homemade treats, you bestow upon your furry companion delectable snacks that nurture their overall health and happiness. With a well-balanced diet and nutritious treats, your dog will revel in a lifetime of vigor and well-being.

The Basics of a Balanced Dog Diet

Ensuring your beloved companion's diet is well-rounded is paramount for their overall vitality and happiness. A balanced diet not only furnishes dogs with vital nutrients but also helps stave off a myriad of health concerns. Familiarizing yourself with the core components of a balanced dog diet will empower you to choose the perfect ingredients for crafting wholesome homemade treats.

Protein serves as a cornerstone in a dog's diet and is indispensable for muscle development, repair, and overall bodily function. Opt for premium protein sources such as lean meats, fish, eggs, and dairy products when concocting homemade treats to fortify your dog's muscle structure and vitality.

Fats stand as another integral part of a balanced diet, furnishing dogs with energy while supporting various physiological processes. Omega-3 and omega-6 fatty acids, sourced from fish oil, flaxseed, and chicken fat, nurture healthy skin, a glossy coat, and cognitive function. Infusing healthy fats into homemade treats ensures your dog receives the essential nutrients for a radiant coat and overall well-being.

Carbohydrates are vital for providing dogs with energy and fiber, promoting digestion and satiety. While dogs are predominantly carnivorous, they can benefit from complex carbohydrates derived from whole grains, fruits, and vegetables. Opt for nourishing options like brown rice, sweet potatoes, and peas in homemade treats to furnish sustained energy sans blood sugar spikes.

Vitamins and minerals are indispensable for bolstering overall health and supporting myriad bodily functions in dogs. Fruits and vegetables abound in vitamins, minerals, and antioxidants that bolster your dog's immune system and vitality. Incorporating a spectrum of colorful fruits and vegetables into homemade treats enriches your dog's diet with a diverse array of nutrients.

When curating ingredients for homemade treats, steer clear of additives, preservatives, and artificial flavors that could compromise your dog's well-being. Instead, opt for natural, whole-food ingredients that are safe and nutritious for canine consumption. Scrutinize labels meticulously and select ingredients devoid of harmful substances.

By mastering the fundamentals of a balanced dog diet and selecting wholesome ingredients for homemade treats, you furnish your furry friend with delectable snacks that promote their overall health and joy. With a balanced diet and nutritious treats, your dog is poised to revel in a lifetime of robust health and well-being.

Understanding Ingredients: What to Use and Why

Delving into the realm of healthy homemade dog treats demands careful ingredient selection. Each component plays a pivotal role in delivering vital nutrients and nurturing your furry companion's overall well-being. Understanding the function of each ingredient empowers you to craft treats that are both nourishing and delectable.

- ✓ **Whole Wheat Flour:** Serving as a cornerstone in many homemade treat recipes, whole wheat flour provides a robust foundation. Laden with carbohydrates for energy and fiber for digestive health, it offers a nutrient-rich alternative to refined flour. However, be mindful of potential wheat allergies, and consider alternatives like brown rice flour or oat flour if needed.
- ✓ **Rolled Oats:** A nutritious boost to homemade treats, rolled oats bring fiber, vitamins, and minerals to the table. Not only do they enhance texture and flavor, but they also support digestive health and bowel regularity, making them an ideal choice for pups with sensitive stomachs.
- ✓ **Peanut Butter:** A canine favorite, peanut butter delights with its rich flavor and creamy texture. Bursting with healthy fats, protein, and essential vitamins, it serves as a wholesome treat option. Ensure you opt for varieties devoid of added sugars, salt, or xylitol, which can pose risks to dogs.
- ✓ **Pumpkin Puree:** Beyond its delicious taste, pumpkin puree packs a nutritional punch. Laden with fiber, vitamins A, C, and E, and antioxidants, it bolsters digestive health, immune function, and overall well-being. Its ability to regulate bowel movements makes it a go-to remedy for digestive woes.
- ✓ **Applesauce:** Unsweetened applesauce infuses natural sweetness and moisture into homemade treats, sans added sugars. Rich in vitamins, fiber, and antioxidants, it supports immune function and aids in healthy digestion. Choose varieties free from added sugars or artificial sweeteners for optimal benefits.
- ✓ **Carrots:** Crunchy and low in calories, carrots are a stellar addition to homemade treats. Abounding in beta-carotene, vitamins A and K, and fiber promote vision, immune function, and digestive health. Their dental benefits make them a popular choice for maintaining oral hygiene.
- ✓ **Chicken:** A lean protein powerhouse, chicken is indispensable for muscle growth, repair, and overall bodily function in dogs. Opt for cooked, boneless, and skinless chicken breast or thighs to minimize fat content and ensure digestibility.

By comprehending the roles of each ingredient and opting for high-quality, nutrient-rich options, you craft homemade dog treats that elevate your furry friend's health and happiness. Explore various combinations and recipes to discover the perfect treats that both satisfy and nourish your beloved companion.

Supplements: Are They Necessary?

In our quest to ensure the well-being of our beloved dogs, the question of whether supplements are necessary often arises among pet owners. While a balanced diet rich in quality ingredients typically meets a dog's nutritional needs, there are instances where supplements can offer added benefits.

- ✓ **Omega-3 Fatty Acids:** Found in fish oil supplements, omega-3 fatty acids are vital for heart health, reducing inflammation, and maintaining healthy skin and coat. While many dog foods contain omega-3s, supplements may be beneficial for dogs with specific skin conditions, joint problems, or allergies.
- ✓ **Glucosamine and Chondroitin:** These supplements support joint health and ease symptoms of arthritis or stiffness, particularly in senior dogs or breeds prone to joint issues. By preserving cartilage integrity and enhancing joint lubrication, they improve mobility and enhance overall quality of life.
- ✓ **Probiotics:** Beneficial bacteria in probiotic supplements bolster digestive health and immune function. They foster a healthy gut microbiome, aid in nutrient absorption, and alleviate digestive ailments like diarrhea or constipation, particularly in dogs with sensitive stomachs or undergoing antibiotic treatment.
- ✓ **Multivitamins:** While a balanced diet usually covers vitamin and mineral needs, some factors may necessitate supplementation. Multivitamins tailored for dogs bridge nutritional gaps, ensuring optimal health, especially for aging dogs or those with specific health conditions.
- ✓ **Antioxidants:** Supplements like vitamin E or C combat free radicals, safeguarding cells from oxidative stress and reducing the risk of chronic diseases. Particularly beneficial for senior dogs or those exposed to environmental toxins, antioxidants support overall health and longevity.

Before incorporating supplements, consulting a veterinarian is paramount. They can evaluate your dog's requirements, suggest suitable supplements, and determine appropriate dosages based on factors like age, breed, size, and health status.

Supplements should complement, not substitute, a balanced diet. Prioritize high-quality, whole-food ingredients and utilize supplements judiciously to address specific health issues or deficiencies.

Ultimately, supplementing your dog's diet should be a thoughtful decision guided by professional advice. With careful consideration and veterinary guidance, supplements can be invaluable in nurturing your dog's health and happiness throughout their life.

Chapter 3: Simple and Basic Treats

Creating homemade dog treats doesn't have to be complicated. Some of the best treats for our furry friends are made with simple, wholesome ingredients that are easy to find and prepare. Below are some delicious recipes for homemade dog treats that are sure to delight your canine companion:

1. Peanut Butter Pup cakes

Ingredients:
- 1 cup whole wheat flour
- 1 teaspoon baking powder
- 1/4 cup peanut butter (unsalted, preferably)
- 1/4 cup unsweetened applesauce
- 1/4 cup water
- 1 egg

Instructions:
- Preheat the oven to 350°F (175°C) and line a mini muffin tin with paper liners.
- In a bowl, mix the whole wheat flour and baking powder.
- In another bowl, whisk together the peanut butter, applesauce, water, and egg until well combined.
- Gradually add the dry ingredients to the wet ingredients, stirring until just combined.
- Spoon the batter into the prepared muffin tin, filling each cup about two-thirds full.
- Bake for 10-12 minutes or until a toothpick inserted into the center comes out clean.
- Allow the pup cakes to cool completely before serving them to your furry friend.

Nutritional Values:
- Calories: 65 per pup cake
- Protein: 2g
- Fat: 3g
- Fiber: 1g

2. Carrot and Oat Dog Biscuits

Ingredients:

- 1 cup rolled oats
- 1/2 cup shredded carrots
- 1/4 cup unsweetened applesauce
- 1 egg

Instructions:

- Preheat the oven to 350°F (175°C) and line a baking sheet with parchment paper.
- In a food processor, pulse the rolled oats until they form a coarse flour-like consistency.
- In a bowl, mix the oat flour, shredded carrots, applesauce, and egg until well combined.
- Roll out the dough on a lightly floured surface to about 1/4-inch thickness.
- Use cookie cutters to cut out shapes or simply slice the dough into squares.
- Place the biscuits on the prepared baking sheet and bake for 15-20 minutes or until golden brown.
- Allow the biscuits to cool completely before serving to your dog.

Nutritional Values:

- Calories: 35 per biscuit
- Protein: 1g
- Fat: 1g
- Fiber: 1g

3. Cheesy Sweet Potato Chews

Ingredients:

- 1 large sweet potato
- 1/4 cup shredded cheddar cheese (unsalted)

Instructions:

- Preheat the oven to 250°F (120°C) and line a baking sheet with parchment paper.
- Wash the sweet potato thoroughly and slice it into thin rounds, about 1/4 inch thick.
- Place the sweet potato slices on the prepared baking sheet, making sure they are not overlapping.
- Sprinkle the shredded cheddar cheese evenly over the sweet potato slices.
- Cook in the oven for 2-3 hours, flipping the slices halfway through until they are dry and somewhat crisp.
- Allow the chews to cool completely before serving to your pup.

Nutritional Values:

- Calories: 20 per chew
- Protein: 1g
- Fat: 1g
- Fiber: 1g

4. Banana and Blueberry Frozen Treats

Ingredients:

- 1 ripe banana
- 1/2 cup fresh blueberries
- 1/2 cup plain yogurt (unsweetened)

Instructions:

- In a blender, combine the ripe banana, fresh blueberries, and plain yogurt.
- Blend until smooth and well combined.
- Pour the mixture into ice cube trays or silicone molds.
- Place the trays or molds in the freezer and freeze until solid, about 2-3 hours.
- Once frozen, remove the treats from the trays or molds and store them in a freezer-safe container.
- Serve these refreshing treats to your dog on hot days for a cool and healthy snack.

Nutritional Values:

- Calories: 15 per treat
- Protein: 1g
- Fat: 0.5g
- Fiber: 1g

5. Chicken and Brown Rice Balls

Ingredients:

- 1 cup cooked brown rice
- 1/2 cup cooked chicken, shredded
- 1/4 cup chicken broth (unsalted)

Instructions:

- In a bowl, mix the cooked brown rice, shredded chicken, and chicken broth until well combined.
- Roll the mixture into small balls about the size of a tablespoon.
- Place the balls on a baking sheet lined with parchment paper.
- Bake in the oven at 350°F (175°C) for 15-20 minutes, or until the balls are firm and golden brown.
- Allow the balls to cool completely before serving to your dog.

Nutritional Values:

- Calories: 25 per ball
- Protein: 2g
- Fat: 1g
- Fiber: 1g

6. Pumpkin and Cinnamon Cookies

Ingredients:

- ✓ 1 cup canned pumpkin (unsweetened)
- ✓ 1 1/2 cups whole wheat flour
- ✓ 1 teaspoon ground cinnamon

Instructions:

- ✓ Preheat the oven to 350°F (175°C) and line a baking sheet with parchment paper.
- ✓ In a bowl, mix the canned pumpkin, whole wheat flour, and ground cinnamon until a dough forms.
- ✓ Roll out the dough on a lightly floured surface to about 1/4-inch thickness.
- ✓ Use cookie cutters to cut out shapes or simply slice the dough into squares.
- ✓ Place the cookies on the prepared baking sheet and bake for 25-30 minutes, or until firm and golden brown.
- ✓ Allow the cookies to cool completely before serving them to your furry friend.

Nutritional Values:

- ✓ Calories: 45 per cookie
- ✓ Protein: 2g
- ✓ Fat: 0.5g
- ✓ Fiber: 2g

7. Salmon and Sweet Potato Sticks

Ingredients:

- 1/2 cup cooked salmon, flaked
- 1/2 cup mashed sweet potato
- 1/4 cup oat flour

Instructions:

- Preheat the oven to 350°F (175°C) and line a baking sheet with parchment paper.
- In a bowl, mix the cooked salmon, mashed sweet potato, and oat flour until well combined.
- Roll the mixture into small sticks about the size of your pinky finger.
- Place the sticks on the prepared baking sheet and bake for 20-25 minutes, or until firm.
- Allow the sticks to cool completely before serving to your dog.

Nutritional Values:

- Calories: 30 per stick
- Protein: 2g
- Fat: 1g
- Fiber: 1g

8. Spinach and Cheese Bites

Ingredients:

- 1 cup cooked spinach, chopped
- 1/2 cup shredded mozzarella cheese (unsalted)
- 1/2 cup oat flour

Instructions:

- Preheat the oven to 350°F (175°C) and line a baking sheet with parchment paper.
- In a bowl, mix the cooked spinach, shredded mozzarella cheese, and oat flour until well combined.
- Roll the mixture into small balls and flatten them slightly onto the prepared baking sheet.
- Bake for 15-20 minutes, or until the bites are set and lightly golden brown.
- Allow the bites to cool completely before serving to your furry friend.

Nutritional Values:

- Calories: 25 per bite
- Protein: 2g
- Fat: 1g
- Fiber: 1g

9. Turkey and Cranberry Jerky

Ingredients:

- 1 cup cooked turkey breast, thinly sliced
- 1/4 cup dried cranberries (unsweetened)

Instructions:

- Preheat the oven to 200°F (95°C) and line a baking sheet with parchment paper.
- Arrange the thinly sliced turkey breast on the prepared baking sheet, making sure the slices are not touching.
- Sprinkle the dried cranberries evenly over the turkey slices.
- Bake in the oven for 2-3 hours, or until the turkey is dried and jerky-like.
- Allow the jerky to cool completely before serving to your dog.

Nutritional Values:

- Calories: 30 per serving (about 2 slices)
- Protein: 3g
- Fat: 0.5g
- Fiber: 0.5g

10. Apple and Cheddar Pup cakes

Ingredients:
- 1 cup grated apple
- 1/2 cup shredded cheddar cheese (unsalted)
- 1/4 cup unsweetened applesauce
- 1/4 cup water
- 1 egg

Instructions:
- Preheat the oven to 350°F (175°C) and line a mini muffin tin with paper liners.
- In a bowl, mix the grated apple, shredded cheddar cheese, applesauce, water, and egg until well combined.
- Gradually add the dry ingredients to the wet ingredients, stirring until just combined.
- Spoon the batter into the prepared muffin tin, filling each cup about two-thirds full.
- Bake for 10-12 minutes or until a toothpick inserted into the center comes out clean.
- Allow the pup cakes to cool completely before serving to your furry friend.

Nutritional Values:
- Calories: 65 per pup cake
- Protein: 2g
- Fat: 3g
- Fiber: 1g

11. Beef and Potato Bites

Ingredients:

- 1/2 cup cooked beef, finely chopped
- 1/2 cup mashed potato
- 1/4 cup oat flour

Instructions:

- Preheat the oven to 350°F (175°C) and line a baking sheet with parchment paper.
- In a bowl, mix the cooked beef, mashed potato, and oat flour until well combined.
- Roll the mixture into small balls and flatten them slightly onto the prepared baking sheet.
- Bake for 15-20 minutes, or until the bites are set and lightly golden brown.
- Allow the bites to cool completely before serving to your furry friend.

Nutritional Values:

- Calories: 25 per bite
- Protein: 2g
- Fat: 1g
- Fiber: 1g

12. Cranberry and Pumpkin Doggy Donuts

Ingredients:
- 1 cup canned pumpkin (unsweetened)
- 1/2 cup dried cranberries (unsweetened)
- 1/4 cup oat flour

Instructions:
- Preheat the oven to 350°F (175°C) and grease a donut pan.
- In a blender or food processor, blend the canned pumpkin and dried cranberries until smooth.
- Transfer the mixture to a bowl and stir in the oat flour until well combined.
- Spoon the mixture into the prepared donut pan, filling each cavity about three-quarters full.
- Bake for 20-25 minutes, or until the donuts are set and lightly golden brown.
- Allow the donuts to cool in the pan for 5 minutes before transferring them to a wire rack to cool completely.

Nutritional Values:
- Calories: 40 per donut
- Protein: 1g
- Fat: 0.5g
- Fiber: 1.5g

13. Turkey Bacon Bites

Ingredients:

- 1/2 cup cooked turkey bacon, finely chopped
- 1/2 cup oat flour
- 1/4 cup unsweetened applesauce

Instructions:

- Preheat the oven to 350°F (175°C) and line a baking sheet with parchment paper.
- In a bowl, mix the cooked turkey bacon, oat flour, and unsweetened applesauce until well combined.
- Roll the mixture into small balls and flatten them slightly onto the prepared baking sheet.
- Bake for 15-20 minutes, or until the bites are set and lightly golden brown.
- Allow the bites to cool completely before serving to your furry friend.

Nutritional Values:

- Calories: 30 per bite
- Protein: 2g
- Fat: 1g
- Fiber: 1g

14. Blueberry and Banana Muffins

Ingredients:
- 1 cup mashed banana
- 1/2 cup fresh blueberries
- 1/4 cup unsweetened applesauce
- 1 egg
- 1 cup oat flour

Instructions:
- Preheat the oven to 350°F (175°C) and line a muffin tin with paper liners.
- In a bowl, mix the mashed banana, fresh blueberries, applesauce, egg, and oat flour until well combined.
- Spoon the batter into the prepared muffin tin, filling each cup about two-thirds full.
- Bake for 20-25 minutes, or until a toothpick inserted into the center comes out clean.
- Allow the muffins to cool completely before serving to your furry friend.

Nutritional Values:
- Calories: 50 per muffin
- Protein: 2g
- Fat: 1g
- Fiber: 2g

15. Cheese and Bacon Twists

Ingredients:

- 1/2 cup shredded cheddar cheese (unsalted)
- 1/4 cup cooked bacon bits, finely chopped
- 1 cup oat flour
- 1/4 cup unsweetened applesauce

Instructions:

- Preheat the oven to 350°F (175°C) and line a baking sheet with parchment paper.
- In a bowl, mix the shredded cheddar cheese, cooked bacon bits, oat flour, and unsweetened applesauce until well combined.
- Roll the mixture into small sticks and twist them gently onto the prepared baking sheet.
- Bake for 15-20 minutes, or until the twists are set and lightly golden brown.
- Allow the twists to cool completely before serving to your furry friend.

Nutritional Values:

- Calories: 30 per twist
- Protein: 2g
- Fat: 1g
- Fiber: 1g

16. Peanut Butter and Banana Frozen Treats

Ingredients:
- 1 ripe banana
- 1/4 cup peanut butter
- 1/2 cup plain yogurt (unsweetened)

Instructions:
- In a blender, combine the ripe banana, peanut butter, and plain yogurt.
- Blend until smooth and well combined.
- Pour the mixture into ice cube trays or silicone molds.
- Place the trays or molds in the freezer and freeze until solid, about 2-3 hours.
- Once frozen, remove the treats from the trays or molds and store them in a freezer-safe container.
- Serve these refreshing treats to your dog on hot days for a cool and healthy snack.

Nutritional Values:
- Calories: 20 per treat
- Protein: 1.5g
- Fat: 1.5g
- Fiber: 1g

17. Liver and Carrot Bites

Ingredients:

- 1/2 cup cooked liver, finely chopped
- 1/2 cup grated carrot
- 1/4 cup oat flour
- 1 egg

Instructions:

- Preheat the oven to 350°F (175°C) and line a baking sheet with parchment paper.
- In a bowl, mix the cooked liver, grated carrot, oat flour, and egg until well combined.
- Roll the mixture into small balls and flatten them slightly onto the prepared baking sheet.
- Bake for 15-20 minutes, or until the bites are set and lightly golden brown.
- Allow the bites to cool completely before serving to your furry friend.

Nutritional Values:

- Calories: 25 per bite
- Protein: 2g
- Fat: 1g
- Fiber: 1g

18. Pumpkin and Peanut Butter Biscuits

Ingredients:

- 1 cup canned pumpkin (unsweetened)
- 1/4 cup peanut butter
- 1 1/2 cups oat flour

Instructions:

- Preheat the oven to 350°F (175°C) and line a baking sheet with parchment paper.
- In a bowl, mix the canned pumpkin and peanut butter until smooth.
- Gradually add the oat flour to the pumpkin mixture, stirring until a dough forms.
- Roll out the dough on a lightly floured surface to about 1/4-inch thickness.
- Use cookie cutters to cut out shapes or simply slice the dough into squares.
- Place the biscuits on the prepared baking sheet and bake for 25-30 minutes or until firm and lightly golden brown.
- Allow the biscuits to cool completely before serving to your dog.

Nutritional Values:

- Calories: 45 per biscuit
- Protein: 2g
- Fat: 1.5g
- Fiber: 2g

19. Turkey and Veggie Meatballs

Ingredients:

- 1/2 cup cooked turkey, finely chopped
- 1/4 cup grated zucchini
- 1/4 cup grated carrot
- 1/4 cup oat flour
- 1 egg

Instructions:

- Preheat the oven to 350°F (175°C) and line a baking sheet with parchment paper.
- In a bowl, mix the cooked turkey, grated zucchini, grated carrot, oat flour, and egg until well combined.
- Roll the mixture into small balls and place them on the prepared baking sheet.
- Bake for 15-20 minutes, or until the meatballs are cooked through and lightly golden brown.
- Allow the meatballs to cool completely before serving to your furry friend.

Nutritional Values:

- Calories: 25 per meatball
- Protein: 2g
- Fat: 1g
- Fiber: 1g

20. Apple and Carrot Crunchies

Ingredients:

- 1 cup grated apple
- 1/2 cup grated carrot
- 1 cup oat flour

Instructions:

- Preheat the oven to 350°F (175°C) and line a baking sheet with parchment paper.
- In a bowl, mix the grated apple, grated carrot, and oat flour until well combined.
- Roll out the dough on a lightly floured surface to about 1/4-inch thickness.
- Use a knife or pizza cutter to slice the dough into small squares or rectangles.
- Place the crunchies on the prepared baking sheet and bake for 20-25 minutes or until crisp and golden brown.
- Allow the crunchies to cool completely before serving to your furry friend.

Nutritional Values:

- Calories: 40 per serving (about 5 crunchies)
- Protein: 1.5g
- Fat: 0.5g
- Fiber: 2g

21. Spinach and Salmon Bites

Ingredients:
- 1/2 cup cooked salmon, flaked
- 1/2 cup cooked spinach, chopped
- 1/4 cup oat flour
- 1 egg

Instructions:
- Preheat the oven to 350°F (175°C) and line a baking sheet with parchment paper.
- In a bowl, mix the cooked salmon, cooked spinach, oat flour, and egg until well combined.
- Roll the mixture into small balls and flatten them slightly onto the prepared baking sheet.
- Bake for 15-20 minutes, or until the bites are set and lightly golden brown.
- Allow the bites to cool completely before serving to your furry friend.

Nutritional Values:
- Calories: 25 per bite
- Protein: 2g
- Fat: 1g
- Fiber: 1g

22. Pumpkin and Carrot Pup cakes

Ingredients:
- 1 cup canned pumpkin (unsweetened)
- 1/2 cup grated carrot
- 1/4 cup unsweetened applesauce
- 1/4 cup water
- 1 egg
- 1 1/2 cups oat flour

Instructions:
- Preheat the oven to 350°F (175°C) and line a mini muffin tin with paper liners.
- In a bowl, mix the canned pumpkin, grated carrot, applesauce, water, egg, and oat flour until well combined.
- Spoon the batter into the prepared muffin tin, filling each cup about two-thirds full.
- Bake for 10-12 minutes or until a toothpick inserted into the center comes out clean.
- Allow the pup cakes to cool completely before serving to your furry friend.

Nutritional Values:
- Calories: 60 per pup cake
- Protein: 2g
- Fat: 1.5g
- Fiber: 2g

23. Turkey and Rice Cookies

Ingredients:
- 1 cup cooked turkey, shredded
- 1 cup cooked brown rice
- 1/4 cup unsweetened applesauce

Instructions:
- Preheat the oven to 350°F (175°C) and line a baking sheet with parchment paper.
- In a bowl, mix the cooked turkey, cooked brown rice, and unsweetened applesauce until well combined.
- Roll out the dough on a lightly floured surface to about 1/4-inch thickness.
- Use cookie cutters to cut out shapes or simply slice the dough into squares.
- Place the cookies on the prepared baking sheet and bake for 25-30 minutes or until firm and lightly golden brown.
- Allow the cookies to cool completely before serving to your furry friend.

Nutritional Values:
- Calories: 40 per cookie
- Protein: 2g
- Fat: 1g
- Fiber: 1g

24. Sweet Potato and Banana Treats

Ingredients:

- 1 cup mashed sweet potato
- 1 ripe banana, mashed
- 1/4 cup unsweetened applesauce
- 1 1/2 cups oat flour

Instructions:

- Preheat the oven to 350°F (175°C) and line a baking sheet with parchment paper.
- In a bowl, mix the mashed sweet potato, mashed banana, applesauce, and oat flour until well combined.
- Roll out the dough on a lightly floured surface to about 1/4-inch thickness.
- Use cookie cutters to cut out shapes or simply slice the dough into squares.
- Place the treats on the prepared baking sheet and bake for 20-25 minutes or until firm and lightly golden brown.
- Allow the treats to cool completely before serving to your furry friend.

Nutritional Values:

- Calories: 50 per treat
- Protein: 2g
- Fat: 1g
- Fiber: 2g

25. Chicken and Pumpkin Poppers

Ingredients:

- 1 cup cooked chicken, shredded
- 1/2 cup canned pumpkin (unsweetened)
- 1/4 cup oat flour
- 1 egg

Instructions:

- Preheat the oven to 350°F (175°C) and line a baking sheet with parchment paper.
- In a bowl, mix the cooked chicken, canned pumpkin, oat flour, and egg until well combined.
- Roll the mixture into small balls and place them on the prepared baking sheet.
- Bake for 15-20 minutes, or until the poppers are set and lightly golden brown.
- Allow the poppers to cool completely before serving to your furry friend.

Nutritional Values:

- Calories: 25 per popper
- Protein: 2g
- Fat: 1g
- Fiber: 1g

26. Blueberry and Coconut Cookies

Ingredients:

- 1 cup fresh blueberries, mashed
- 1/2 cup shredded unsweetened coconut
- 1/4 cup unsweetened applesauce
- 1 1/2 cups oat flour

Instructions:

- Preheat the oven to 350°F (175°C) and line a baking sheet with parchment paper.
- In a bowl, mix the mashed blueberries, shredded coconut, applesauce, and oat flour until well combined.
- Roll out the dough on a lightly floured surface to about 1/4-inch thickness.
- Use cookie cutters to cut out shapes or simply slice the dough into squares.
- Place the cookies on the prepared baking sheet and bake for 25-30 minutes or until firm and lightly golden brown.
- Allow the cookies to cool completely before serving to your furry friend.

Nutritional Values:

- Calories: 45 per cookie
- Protein: 1.5g
- Fat: 1.5g
- Fiber: 2g

27. Liver and Oatmeal Biscuits

Ingredients:

- 1/2 cup cooked liver, finely chopped
- 1/4 cup unsweetened applesauce
- 1 1/2 cups oat flour

Instructions:

- Preheat the oven to 350°F (175°C) and line a baking sheet with parchment paper.
- In a bowl, mix the cooked liver, applesauce, and oat flour until well combined.
- Roll out the dough on a lightly floured surface to about 1/4-inch thickness.
- Use cookie cutters to cut out shapes or simply slice the dough into squares.
- Place the biscuits on the prepared baking sheet and bake for 25-30 minutes or until firm and lightly golden brown.
- Allow the biscuits to cool completely before serving to your furry friend.

Nutritional Values:

- Calories: 40 per biscuit
- Protein: 2g
- Fat: 1g
- Fiber: 2g

28. Turkey and Cranberry Poppers

Ingredients:

- 1 cup cooked turkey, shredded
- 1/4 cup dried cranberries (unsweetened)
- 1/4 cup oat flour
- 1 egg

Instructions:

- Preheat the oven to 350°F (175°C) and line a baking sheet with parchment paper.
- In a bowl, mix the cooked turkey, dried cranberries, oat flour, and egg until well combined.
- Roll the mixture into small balls and place them on the prepared baking sheet.
- Bake for 15-20 minutes, or until the poppers are set and lightly golden brown.
- Allow the poppers to cool completely before serving to your furry friend.

Nutritional Values:

- Calories: 30 per popper
- Protein: 2g
- Fat: 1g
- Fiber: 1g

29. Carrot and Peanut Butter Cookies

Ingredients:

- 1 cup grated carrot
- 1/4 cup unsweetened applesauce
- 1/4 cup peanut butter
- 1 1/2 cups oat flour

Instructions:

- Preheat the oven to 350°F (175°C) and line a baking sheet with parchment paper.
- In a bowl, mix the grated carrot, applesauce, peanut butter, and oat flour until well combined.
- Roll out the dough on a lightly floured surface to about 1/4-inch thickness.
- Use cookie cutters to cut out shapes or simply slice the dough into squares.
- Place the cookies on a prepared baking sheet and leave them in the oven for 25 to 30 minutes, or until they are firm and have a slightly golden hue.
- Allow the cookies to cool completely before serving to your furry friend.

Nutritional Values:

- Calories: 45 per cookie
- Protein: 2g
- Fat: 1.5g
- Fiber: 2g

30. Banana and Peanut Butter Frozen Pops

Ingredients:
- 1 ripe banana
- 1/4 cup peanut butter
- 1/2 cup plain yogurt (unsweetened)

Instructions:
- In a blender, combine the ripe banana, peanut butter, and plain yogurt.
- Blend until smooth and well combined.
- Pour the mixture into ice cube trays or silicone molds.
- Place the trays or molds in the freezer and freeze until solid, about 2-3 hours.
- Once frozen, remove the pops from the trays or molds and store them in a freezer-safe container.
- Serve these refreshing pops to your dog on hot days for a cool and healthy snack.

Nutritional Values:
- Calories: 20 per pop
- Protein: 1.5g
- Fat: 1.5g
- Fiber: 1g

31. Apple and Cheddar Biscuits

Ingredients:

- 1 cup grated apple
- 1/2 cup shredded cheddar cheese (unsalted)
- 1/4 cup unsweetened applesauce
- 1 1/2 cups oat flour

Instructions:

- Preheat the oven to 350°F (175°C) and line a baking sheet with parchment paper.
- In a bowl, mix the grated apple, shredded cheddar cheese, applesauce, and oat flour until well combined.
- Roll out the dough on a lightly floured surface to about 1/4-inch thickness.
- Use cookie cutters to cut out shapes or simply slice the dough into squares.
- Place the biscuits on the prepared baking sheet and bake for 25-30 minutes or until firm and lightly golden brown.
- Allow the biscuits to cool completely before serving to your furry friend.

Nutritional Values:

- Calories: 50 per biscuit
- Protein: 2g
- Fat: 1.5g
- Fiber: 2g

32. Peanut Butter and Jelly Bites

Ingredients:
- 1/4 cup peanut butter
- 1/4 cup unsweetened applesauce
- 1/4 cup oat flour
- 1/4 cup low-sugar fruit jam (such as raspberry or strawberry)

Instructions:
- Preheat the oven to 350°F (175°C) and line a baking sheet with parchment paper.
- In a bowl, mix the peanut butter, applesauce, and oat flour until well combined.
- Roll the mixture into small balls and place them on the prepared baking sheet.
- Using your thumb or the back of a spoon, make an indentation in the center of each ball.
- Fill each indentation with a small amount of fruit jam.
- Bake for 10-12 minutes, or until the bites are set.
- Allow the bites to cool completely before serving to your furry friend.

Nutritional Values:
- Calories: 30 per bite
- Protein: 1g
- Fat: 1.5g
- Fiber: 1g

33. Turkey and Vegetable Patties

Ingredients:

- 1 cup cooked turkey, shredded
- 1/2 cup grated zucchini
- 1/4 cup grated carrot
- 1/4 cup oat flour
- 1 egg

Instructions:

- Preheat the oven to 350°F (175°C) and line a baking sheet with parchment paper.
- In a bowl, mix the cooked turkey, grated zucchini, grated carrot, oat flour, and egg until well combined.
- Form the mixture into small patties and place them on the prepared baking sheet.
- Bake for 15-20 minutes, or until the patties are cooked through and lightly golden brown.
- Allow the patties to cool completely before serving to your furry friend.

Nutritional Values:

- Calories: 35 per patty
- Protein: 2g
- Fat: 1g
- Fiber: 1g

34. Blueberry and Banana Pup Pops

Ingredients:
- 1 ripe banana
- 1/2 cup fresh blueberries
- 1/2 cup plain yogurt (unsweetened)
- 1/4 cup water

Instructions:
- In a blender, combine the ripe banana, fresh blueberries, plain yogurt, and water.
- Blend until smooth and well combined.
- Pour the mixture into ice cube trays or silicone molds.
- Place the trays or molds in the freezer and freeze until solid, about 2-3 hours.
- Once frozen, remove the pops from the trays or molds and store them in a freezer-safe container.
- Serve these refreshing pops to your dog on hot days for a cool and healthy snack.

Nutritional Values:
- Calories: 20 per pop
- Protein: 1g
- Fat: 0.5g
- Fiber: 1g

35. Chicken and Spinach Balls

Ingredients:

- 1 cup cooked chicken, shredded
- 1/2 cup cooked spinach, chopped
- 1/4 cup oat flour
- 1 egg

Instructions:

- Preheat the oven to 350°F (175°C) and line a baking sheet with parchment paper.
- In a bowl, mix the cooked chicken, cooked spinach, oat flour, and egg until well combined.
- Roll the mixture into small balls and place them on the prepared baking sheet.
- Bake for 15-20 minutes, or until the balls are set and lightly golden brown.
- Allow the balls to cool completely before serving to your furry friend.

Nutritional Values:

- Calories: 30 per ball
- Protein: 2g
- Fat: 1g
- Fiber: 1g

36. Carrot and Zucchini Chips

Ingredients:

- 1 large carrot, thinly sliced
- 1 small zucchini, thinly sliced
- 1 tablespoon olive oil

Instructions:

- Preheat the oven to 250°F (120°C) and line a baking sheet with parchment paper.
- In a bowl, toss the thinly sliced carrot and zucchini with olive oil until evenly coated.
- Spread the slices in a single layer on the prepared baking sheet.
- Bake for 2-3 hours, flipping the slices halfway through, until they are dried and slightly crispy.
- Allow the chips to cool completely before serving your pup.

Nutritional Values:

- Calories: 15 per serving (about 10 chips)
- Protein: 0.5g
- Fat: 1g
- Fiber: 1g

37. Salmon and Sweet Potato Balls

Ingredients:

- 1 cup cooked salmon, flaked
- 1/2 cup mashed sweet potato
- 1/4 cup oat flour
- 1 egg

Instructions:

- Preheat the oven to 350°F (175°C) and line a baking sheet with parchment paper.
- In a bowl, mix the cooked salmon, mashed sweet potato, oat flour, and egg until well combined.
- Roll the mixture into small balls and place them on the prepared baking sheet.
- Bake for 15-20 minutes, or until the balls are cooked through and lightly golden brown.
- Allow the balls to cool completely before serving to your furry friend.

Nutritional Values:

- Calories: 30 per ball
- Protein: 2g
- Fat: 1g
- Fiber: 1g

38. Banana and Carrot Biscotti

Ingredients:

- 1 ripe banana
- 1/2 cup grated carrot
- 1/4 cup unsweetened applesauce
- 1 1/2 cups oat flour

Instructions:

- Preheat the oven to 350°F (175°C) and line a baking sheet with parchment paper.
- In a bowl, mix the ripe banana, grated carrot, applesauce, and oat flour until well combined.
- Form the dough into a log shape on the prepared baking sheet.
- Bake for 25-30 minutes or until firm and lightly golden brown.
- Remove from the oven and let it cool for 10 minutes.
- Using a sharp knife, slice the log into biscotti-sized pieces.
- Place the slices back on the baking sheet and bake for an additional 10-15 minutes, or until crisp.
- Allow the biscotti to cool completely before serving to your furry friend.

Nutritional Values:

- Calories: 40 per biscotti
- Protein: 2g
- Fat: 1.5g
- Fiber: 2g

39. Turkey and Quinoa Balls

Ingredients:

- 1 cup cooked turkey, shredded
- 1/2 cup cooked quinoa
- 1/4 cup oat flour
- 1 egg

Instructions:

- Preheat the oven to 350°F (175°C) and line a baking sheet with parchment paper.
- In a bowl, mix the cooked turkey, cooked quinoa, oat flour, and egg until well combined.
- Roll the mixture into small balls and place them on the prepared baking sheet.
- Bake for 15-20 minutes, or until the balls are cooked through and lightly golden brown.
- Allow the balls to cool completely before serving to your furry friend.

Nutritional Values:

- Calories: 30 per ball
- Protein: 2g
- Fat: 1g
- Fiber: 1g

40. Pumpkin and Cinnamon Twists

Ingredients:

- 1/2 cup canned pumpkin (unsweetened)
- 1 teaspoon ground cinnamon
- 1 1/2 cups oat flour

Instructions:

- Preheat the oven to 350°F (175°C) and line a baking sheet with parchment paper.
- In a bowl, mix the canned pumpkin and ground cinnamon until well combined.
- Gradually add the oat flour to the pumpkin mixture, stirring until a dough forms.
- Roll out the dough on a lightly floured surface to about 1/4 inch thickness.
- Cut the dough into strips and twist them gently onto the prepared baking sheet.
- Bake for 15-20 minutes, or until the twists are set and lightly golden brown.
- Allow the twists to cool completely before serving to your furry friend.

Nutritional Values:

- Calories: 40 per twist
- Protein: 1.5g
- Fat: 0.5g
- Fiber: 2g

41. Cheese and Parsley Biscuits

Ingredients:

- 1/2 cup shredded cheddar cheese (unsalted)
- 1 tablespoon fresh parsley, chopped
- 1/4 cup unsweetened applesauce
- 1 1/2 cups oat flour

Instructions:

- Preheat the oven to 350°F (175°C) and line a baking sheet with parchment paper.
- In a bowl, mix the shredded cheddar cheese, chopped parsley, applesauce, and oat flour until well combined.
- Roll out the dough on a lightly floured surface to about 1/4-inch thickness.
- Use cookie cutters to cut out shapes or simply slice the dough into squares.
- Place the biscuits on the prepared baking sheet and bake for 25-30 minutes or until firm and lightly golden brown.
- Allow the biscuits to cool completely before serving to your furry friend.

Nutritional Values:

- Calories: 45 per biscuit
- Protein: 2g
- Fat: 1.5g
- Fiber: 2g

42. Pumpkin and Peanut Butter Bites

Ingredients:

- 1/2 cup canned pumpkin (unsweetened)
- 1/4 cup peanut butter
- 1/4 cup unsweetened applesauce
- 1 1/2 cups oat flour

Instructions:

- Preheat the oven to 350°F (175°C) and line a baking sheet with parchment paper.
- In a bowl, mix the canned pumpkin, peanut butter, applesauce, and oat flour until well combined.
- Roll the mixture into small balls and place them on the prepared baking sheet.
- Flatten each ball with a fork to create a cookie shape.
- Bake for 15-20 minutes, or until the bites are set and lightly golden brown.
- Allow the bites to cool completely before serving to your furry friend.

Nutritional Values:

- Calories: 40 per bite
- Protein: 2g
- Fat: 1.5g
- Fiber: 2g

43. Chicken and Carrot Cookies

Ingredients:

- 1 cup cooked chicken, shredded
- 1/2 cup grated carrot
- 1/4 cup unsweetened applesauce
- 1 1/2 cups oat flour

Instructions:

- Preheat the oven to 350°F (175°C) and line a baking sheet with parchment paper.
- In a bowl, mix the cooked chicken, grated carrot, applesauce, and oat flour until well combined.
- Roll out the dough on a lightly floured surface to about 1/4-inch thickness.
- Use cookie cutters to cut out shapes or simply slice the dough into squares.
- Place the cookies on the prepared baking sheet and bake them for 25 to 30 minutes, or until they are firm and have turned a light golden color.
- Allow the cookies to cool completely before serving to your furry friend.

Nutritional Values:

- Calories: 45 per cookie
- Protein: 2g
- Fat: 1.5g
- Fiber: 2g

44. Blueberry and Banana Twists

Ingredients:

- 1 ripe banana
- 1/2 cup fresh blueberries
- 1/4 cup unsweetened applesauce
- 1 1/2 cups oat flour

Instructions:

- Preheat the oven to 350°F (175°C) and line a baking sheet with parchment paper.
- In a blender or food processor, blend the ripe banana, fresh blueberries, and applesauce until smooth.
- Transfer the mixture to a bowl and gradually add the oat flour, stirring until a dough forms.
- Roll out the dough on a lightly floured surface to about 1/4-inch thickness.
- Cut the dough into strips and twist them gently onto the prepared baking sheet.
- Bake for 15-20 minutes, or until the twists are set and lightly golden brown.
- Allow the twists to cool completely before serving to your furry friend.

Nutritional Values:

- Calories: 50 per twist
- Protein: 1.5g
- Fat: 1g
- Fiber: 2g

45. Turkey and Cranberry Cookies

Ingredients:

- 1 cup cooked turkey, shredded
- 1/4 cup dried cranberries (unsweetened)
- 1/4 cup unsweetened applesauce
- 1 1/2 cups oat flour

Instructions:

- Preheat the oven to 350°F (175°C) and line a baking sheet with parchment paper.
- In a bowl, mix the cooked turkey, dried cranberries, applesauce, and oat flour until well combined.
- Roll out the dough on a lightly floured surface to about 1/4-inch thickness.
- Use cookie cutters to cut out shapes or simply slice the dough into squares.
- Place the cookies on the prepared baking sheet and bake for 25-30 minutes or until firm and lightly golden brown.
- Allow the cookies to cool completely before serving to your furry friend.

Nutritional Values:

- Calories: 45 per cookie
- Protein: 2g
- Fat: 1.5g
- Fiber: 2g

46. Spinach and Feta Bites

Ingredients:

- 1/2 cup cooked spinach, chopped
- 1/4 cup crumbled feta cheese (unsalted)
- 1/4 cup unsweetened applesauce
- 1 1/2 cups oat flour

Instructions:

- Preheat the oven to 350°F (175°C) and line a baking sheet with parchment paper.
- In a bowl, mix the cooked spinach, crumbled feta cheese, applesauce, and oat flour until well combined.
- Roll the mixture into small balls and place them on the prepared baking sheet.
- Flatten each ball slightly with the back of a spoon.
- Bake for 15-20 minutes, or until the bites are set and lightly golden brown.
- Allow the bites to cool completely before serving to your furry friend.

Nutritional Values:

- Calories: 40 per bite
- Protein: 2g
- Fat: 1.5g
- Fiber: 2g

47. Carrot and Apple Chips

Ingredients:

- 1 large carrot, thinly sliced
- 1 apple, thinly sliced
- 1 tablespoon olive oil

Instructions:

- Preheat the oven to 250°F (120°C) and line a baking sheet with parchment paper.
- In a bowl, toss the thinly sliced carrot and apple with olive oil until evenly coated.
- Spread the slices in a single layer on the prepared baking sheet.
- Bake for 2-3 hours, flipping the slices halfway through, until they are dried and slightly crispy.
- Allow the chips to cool completely before serving your pup.

Nutritional Values:

- Calories: 20 per serving (about 10 chips)
- Protein: 0.5g
- Fat: 1g
- Fiber: 1g

48. Turkey and Sweet Potato Muffins

Ingredients:

- 1 cup cooked turkey, shredded
- 1/2 cup mashed sweet potato
- 1/4 cup unsweetened applesauce
- 1/4 cup water
- 1 egg
- 1 1/2 cups oat flour

Instructions:

- Preheat the oven to 350°F (175°C) and line a muffin tin with paper liners.
- In a bowl, mix the cooked turkey, mashed sweet potato, applesauce, water, egg, and oat flour until well combined.
- Spoon the batter into the prepared muffin tin, filling each cup about two-thirds full.
- Bake for 15-20 minutes or until a toothpick inserted into the center comes out clean.
- Allow the muffins to cool completely before serving them to your furry friend.

Nutritional Values:

- Calories: 55 per muffin
- Protein: 2.5g
- Fat: 1.5g
- Fiber: 2g

49. Chicken and Cheese Balls

Ingredients:

- 1 cup cooked chicken, shredded
- 1/4 cup shredded cheddar cheese (unsalted)
- 1/4 cup unsweetened applesauce
- 1 1/2 cups oat flour

Instructions:

- Preheat the oven to 350°F (175°C) and line a baking sheet with parchment paper.
- In a bowl, mix the cooked chicken, shredded cheddar cheese, applesauce, and oat flour until well combined.
- Roll the mixture into small balls and place them on the prepared baking sheet.
- Bake for 15-20 minutes, or until the balls are set and lightly golden brown.
- Allow the balls to cool completely before serving to your furry friend.

Nutritional Values:

- Calories: 50 per ball
- Protein: 2g
- Fat: 1.5g
- Fiber: 2g

50. Blueberry and Carrot Muffins

Ingredients:

- 1/2 cup fresh blueberries
- 1/2 cup grated carrot
- 1/4 cup unsweetened applesauce
- 1/4 cup water
- 1 egg
- 1 1/2 cups oat flour

Instructions:

- Preheat the oven to 350°F (175°C) and line a muffin tin with paper liners.
- In a bowl, mix the fresh blueberries, grated carrot, applesauce, water, egg, and oat flour until well combined.
- Spoon the batter into the prepared muffin tin, filling each cup about two-thirds full.
- Bake for 15-20 minutes or until a toothpick inserted into the center comes out clean.
- Allow the muffins to cool completely before serving to your furry friend.

Nutritional Values:

- Calories: 50 per muffin
- Protein: 2g
- Fat: 1g
- Fiber: 2g

Introduction to Easy Recipes

In the world of homemade dog treats, simplicity takes center stage. Crafting nutritious and tasty snacks for your furry companion doesn't need to be complex or time-consuming. With straightforward recipes and a handful of basic ingredients, you can whip up treats that will make your dog's tail wag with joy.

Keeping it simple is the golden rule when making homemade dog treats. Minimal ingredients and easy-to-follow instructions ensure that your treats are not only delicious but also packed with goodness. Whether you're a kitchen expert or a beginner, these recipes are designed to be accessible to everyone.

The beauty of easy recipes lies in their adaptability. From simple biscuits to flavorful delights, there's a wide variety of treats you can create using just a few ingredients. Whether your dog craves savory or sweet, there's something to suit every taste.

Not only are easy recipes convenient for busy pet owners, but they also offer room for creativity and personalization. Feel free to experiment with different ingredients, flavors, and textures to tailor the treats to your dog's preferences. Whether it's swapping peanut butter for almond butter or adding extra fruits and veggies, the options are endless.

Aside from simplicity and customization, easy recipes provide peace of mind regarding ingredient quality. By using whole, natural ingredients, you can ensure that your dog receives top-notch nutrition without any unnecessary additives or preservatives. Homemade treats also give you full control over ingredients, allowing you to avoid potential allergens or fillers.

Making homemade dog treats isn't just about the end product—it's also about the bond it creates between you and your pet. Spending time together in the kitchen, preparing delicious snacks for your furry friend, strengthens your relationship and creates cherished memories. And seeing the sheer joy on your dog's face as they enjoy their homemade treats is simply priceless.

In this section of the book, you'll discover a collection of easy recipes perfect for any occasion. Whether you need a quick snack or a special treat to mark an event, these recipes are guaranteed to please your four-legged friend. Each recipe is thoughtfully crafted to meet the nutritional needs outlined in this book, ensuring your dog gets the balanced diet they deserve.

So, roll up your sleeves, fire up the oven, and get ready for a delightful culinary journey with your furry pal. With these easy recipes in hand, store-bought treats will be a thing of the past.

Single-Ingredient Wonders

In the world of homemade dog treats, simplicity is often the key to success. Single-ingredient treats not only simplify the cooking process but also offer numerous health benefits for our beloved pets. Let's explore some of these single-ingredient wonders that are guaranteed to bring joy to your furry friend.

Sweet Potato Chews are a nutritional powerhouse for dogs, packed with essential vitamins, minerals, and fiber. Simply slice sweet potatoes into thin strips, bake them until chewy, and watch as your dog happily munches away on this delicious treat.

Frozen Banana Bites are both tasty and nutritious, providing a rich source of potassium, vitamins, and antioxidants. Freeze bite-sized banana pieces on a baking sheet until firm for a refreshing and satisfying snack, perfect for warm summer days.

Carrot Crunchers are a crunchy delight, favored by many dogs for their low-calorie, high-fiber content, and rich vitamin profile. Simply slice carrots into bite-sized pieces for a nutritious and satisfying treat.

Apple Slices offer a nutritious option, brimming with vitamins A and C, along with fiber to aid digestion. Remove the core and seeds, then slice apples into wedges for a wholesome snack your dog will adore.

Green Beans are another favorite among dogs, providing a low-calorie, high-fiber option packed with essential vitamins and minerals. Steam or blanch fresh green beans until tender, then cool and serve for a healthy treat.

Blueberry Delights are bursting with antioxidants and vitamins, promoting heart health and cognitive function in dogs. Simply wash fresh blueberries and offer them as a delicious and nutritious snack.

Pumpkin Puree is a fiber-rich, low-calorie addition to your dog's diet, boasting vitamins A, C, and E, along with potassium and iron. Spoon some canned pumpkin puree into your dog's bowl for a tasty and beneficial treat.

These single-ingredient wonders not only simplify treat-making but also offer a plethora of health benefits for your furry companion. Whether you opt for a crunchy carrot or a frozen banana bite, these simple recipes are sure to delight even the most discerning pups. Give them a try and witness the joy they bring to your dog's life!

Basic Biscuits and Chews

In the realm of homemade dog treats, simple biscuits, and chews hold a special place. These uncomplicated yet gratifying snacks are not only a breeze to prepare but also offer a crunchy texture that many dogs adore. Below, we've curated a selection of original recipes that are bound to become household favorites.

- ✓ **Peanut Butter Biscuits:** A timeless favorite among canines, these biscuits require only four basic ingredients – whole wheat flour, peanut butter, eggs, and water. With the addition of creamy peanut butter, these treats boast a rich flavor that will have your pup begging for more.
- ✓ **Cheese Biscuits:** Tailored for cheese enthusiasts, these savory treats feature shredded cheddar cheese, whole wheat flour, and eggs. Bursting with flavor and nutrients, these biscuits are effortlessly prepared – simply mix, roll out the dough, cut into shapes, and bake.
- ✓ **Oatmeal Chews:** Catering to dogs with sensitive stomachs, these gentle and nutritious chews are crafted from rolled oats, applesauce, and a hint of cinnamon. Easy to digest and rich in fiber, they offer a wholesome alternative to store-bought rawhide chews.
- ✓ **Pumpkin Spice Biscuits:** Ideal for autumn or anytime your pup craves a festive treat, these biscuits infuse canned pumpkin with whole wheat flour, eggs, and a sprinkle of cinnamon and nutmeg. Nutritious and flavorful, they provide a fiber and vitamin boost.
- ✓ **Carrot and Apple Biscuits:** Perfect for dogs with a sweet tooth, these fruity biscuits combine grated carrots, applesauce, whole wheat flour, and eggs. Packed with essential vitamins and minerals, their natural sweetness eliminates the need for added sugars.
- ✓ **Chicken and Rice Biscuits:** Tailored for savory preferences, these biscuits feature cooked chicken breast, brown rice flour, and eggs. Protein-rich and easily digestible, they offer a delectable way to utilize leftover chicken from your meals.
- ✓ **Beef Jerky Chews:** Satisfying the cravings of meat-loving dogs, these chews combine lean beef, soy sauce, and a touch of honey. Bursting with flavor and protein, they offer a healthier alternative to store-bought jerky treats.

These basic biscuits and chews are not only scrumptious but also simple to prepare, brimming with wholesome ingredients. With just a few straightforward steps, you can whip up a batch of homemade treats that will undoubtedly bring joy to your furry friend's life. So why not give them a try and witness the happiness they bring?

"I hope you are finding the recipes in this book both fun and beneficial for your furry friend! If you've started experimenting with the treats, I would greatly appreciate it if you took a moment to leave a review on Amazon. Your insights could greatly help other pet owners in their quest for healthier dog treat options, and it would be immensely rewarding for me to know how this book has impacted your dog treat adventures. Your support in sharing your experience is invaluable—thank you!"

Chapter 4: Special Dietary Needs

Every dog is as unique as their personality, and some may have specific dietary requirements or restrictions stemming from allergies, sensitivities, or health conditions. When crafting homemade dog treats, it's crucial to consider these individual needs to ensure that every furry friend can indulge in a delicious and safe snack. Here are some valuable tips for accommodating special dietary needs in your homemade treats:

- ✓ **Grain-Free Options:** Many dogs face allergies or sensitivities to grains like wheat, corn, or rice. To cater to these pups, explore alternative flours such as coconut flour, almond flour, or chickpea flour in your recipes. These grain-free alternatives retain both taste and nutrition while being gentle on sensitive stomachs.
- ✓ **Limited Ingredient Recipes:** For dogs with food allergies or sensitivities, simplicity is key. Opt for recipes featuring only a few wholesome ingredients, such as lean proteins like chicken or turkey, and easily digestible carbohydrates like sweet potatoes or pumpkin. Steer clear of common allergens like dairy, soy, or artificial additives.
- ✓ **Hypoallergenic Treats:** Some dogs may require hypoallergenic treats specially designed to minimize allergic reactions. Seek out recipes utilizing novel protein sources such as venison, duck, or rabbit, as these are less likely to trigger sensitivities. Additionally, avoid ingredients known to cause allergic responses, such as beef, chicken, or dairy.
- ✓ **Low-Fat Options:** Dogs with conditions like pancreatitis or digestive issues may need low-fat treats to manage their health effectively. Look for recipes incorporating lean proteins and limiting added fats like oils or butter. Opt for lean cuts of meat and steer clear of fatty ingredients such as cheese or bacon.
- ✓ **High-Fiber Treats:** Dogs grappling with digestive problems or weight management concerns can benefit from high-fiber treats. Integrate ingredients like pumpkin, sweet potatoes, carrots, and green beans into your recipes to elevate fiber content. These components not only aid digestion but also promote a feeling of fullness and satisfaction.

By considering these special dietary needs, you can ensure that every dog can savor homemade treats that marry deliciousness with nutritional value. Whether your pup requires grain-free alternatives, limited ingredient recipes, hypoallergenic options, low-fat treats, or high-fiber snacks, there exists a plethora of homemade treat recipes tailored to meet their unique requirements.

Grain-Free Treats

For dogs with grain allergies or sensitivities, grain-free treats provide a delectable alternative while still delivering essential nutrients. These recipes prioritize simple, wholesome ingredients devoid of grains like wheat, corn, or rice. Here are some inventive and nutritious grain-free treat options tailored for your furry companion:

- ✓ **Salmon and Sweet Potato Bites:** Packed with protein and healthy fats from salmon, these treats are ideal for grain-sensitive dogs. Blend canned salmon, mashed sweet potatoes, and coconut flour into a dough, then shape into bite-sized pieces. Bake until crisp and golden for a savory snack that's bound to be a hit.
- ✓ **Coconut and Blueberry Balls:** Coconut flour, inherently grain-free, infuses these treats with a delightful tropical twist. Combine coconut flour with shredded coconut, fresh blueberries, and a dash of coconut oil to form a dough. Roll into balls and refrigerate until firm, offering your pup a refreshing and nutrient-packed snack.
- ✓ **Turkey and Pumpkin Cookies:** Turkey, a lean protein source gentle on sensitive stomachs, shines in these grain-free delights. Mix ground turkey with pumpkin puree, almond flour, and a hint of cinnamon to create a dough. Shape into cookies and bake until firm, providing your furry friend with a savory and satisfying treat.
- ✓ **Peanut Butter and Banana Squares:** Dogs adore the classic combo of peanut butter and bananas. Blend mashed bananas with peanut butter, almond flour, and a touch of honey to form a dough. Press into a baking pan and bake until golden brown. Once cooled, slice into squares for a sweet and wholesome indulgence.
- ✓ **Beef and Carrot Jerky:** Homemade jerky offers a straightforward and nutritious option, particularly for dogs with grain allergies. Thinly slice lean beef and toss with grated carrots, apple cider vinegar, and a sprinkle of turmeric. Dehydrate until fully dried, providing a chewy and flavorful snack free from grains and artificial additives.

These grain-free treat recipes not only tantalize the taste buds but also cater to dogs with unique dietary requirements. With their wholesome ingredients and irresistible flavors, they're destined to become staples in your pup's treat repertoire.

Low-Calorie Snacks

For dogs requiring weight management or those keeping an eye on their calorie intake, opting for low-calorie snacks ensures a healthy and satisfying indulgence. These treats are thoughtfully crafted to deliver flavor and nutrition without the excess calories. Here are some uncomplicated yet delightful low-calorie snack concepts tailored for your furry friend:

- **Crunchy Carrot Bites:** Carrots, rich in fiber and low in calories, are an ideal choice for weight-conscious dogs. Slice carrots into bite-sized pieces and bake until crispy. These crunchy treats not only promote dental health but also satiate your pup's chewing instincts.
- **Tender Green Bean Morsels:** Green beans, another low-calorie option, offer a satisfying crunch for dogs. Steam or blanch fresh green beans until tender yet crisp, then allow them to cool. These nutritious snacks are perfect for both a light treat and hydration.
- **Refreshing Apple Wedges:** Naturally sweet and low in calories, apples make a wholesome snack for dogs. Slice apples into wedges, removing the core and seeds, before serving. Ensure to eliminate the seeds, as they can pose a hazard. These apple slices provide hydration and a burst of flavor.
- **Frozen Yogurt Bites:** Plain, unsweetened yogurt boasts low calories and beneficial probiotics for digestive health. Spoon small portions of yogurt onto parchment paper-lined baking sheets and freeze until solid. These frozen yogurt bites offer a cool and creamy refreshment for your furry companion.
- **Crispy Zucchini Chips:** Zucchini, a low-calorie vegetable, can be transformed into delightful chips for your pup. Slice zucchini thinly and bake until crispy. These zucchini chips offer a light and satisfying crunch that's perfect for weight-conscious dogs.

These low-calorie snack ideas not only tantalize your dog's taste buds but also provide essential nutrients like vitamins, minerals, and fiber. By incorporating these treats into your pup's routine, you can help them maintain a healthy weight while ensuring they enjoy delicious snacks.

Hypoallergenic Options

For dogs grappling with food sensitivities or allergies, sourcing suitable treats can prove daunting. Hypoallergenic options center around ingredients that are less likely to incite allergic reactions, offering a secure and delightful snack for sensitive pups. Here's a lineup of hypoallergenic treat ideas to ponder:

- ✓ **Turkey and Oat Biscuits:** Turkey, often well-received by dogs with allergies, pairs seamlessly with oats, a nutritious and hypoallergenic grain. Blend ground turkey with oat flour, a hint of olive oil, and a splash of water to create a dough. Fashion the dough into biscuit shapes and bake until golden brown and crunchy.
- ✓ **Quinoa and Spinach Balls:** Quinoa, a gluten-free grain rich in protein, harmonizes well with delicate spinach. Combine cooked quinoa with finely chopped spinach, a beaten egg, and a sprinkle of nutritional yeast. Mold the mixture into balls and bake until firm, yielding a delectable and hypoallergenic treat.
- ✓ **Coconut and Pumpkin Bites:** Harness the benefits of coconut and pumpkin, both hypoallergenic ingredients, boasting numerous health perks. Blend coconut flour with pumpkin puree, coconut oil, and a dash of cinnamon to form a dough. Shape the dough into bite-sized pieces and bake until lightly golden for a flavorful and hypoallergenic delight.
- ✓ **Lamb and Pea Cookies:** Lamb, a novel protein source less likely to incite allergic reactions, pairs exquisitely with pureed peas. Mix ground lamb with pea puree, a hint of parsley, and a drizzle of honey for sweetness. Sculpt the mixture into cookies and bake until cooked through, yielding savory and hypoallergenic treats.
- ✓ **Sweet Potato and Salmon Squares:** Embrace the digestibility of sweet potatoes and salmon, offering an unlikely duo of allergy triggers. Mash cooked sweet potatoes with canned salmon, a touch of coconut flour, and a sprinkle of dried dill. Press the mixture into a baking dish and bake until set, delivering a nutritious and hypoallergenic snack.

These allergy-friendly treat alternatives furnish a delicious and risk-free option for dogs with dietary sensitivities, granting them the joy of indulging in tasty snacks sans apprehension. By thoughtfully selecting ingredients, you can furnish your pup with wholesome treats, fostering their health and happiness.

Chapter 5: Training Treats and Rewards

Training your dog is a pivotal aspect of fostering a strong bond and safeguarding their welfare. Treats serve as a cornerstone in positive reinforcement training, incentivizing your furry companion to grasp new behaviors and commands. When selecting training treats, prioritize small, bite-sized snacks that are easily consumable and won't satiate your dog too quickly. Here are several homemade training treat concepts ideal for rewarding your pup during training sessions:

- ✓ **Chicken Liver Bites:** Chicken liver, abundant in palatability and protein, ranks high among canine favorites. Slice raw chicken liver into petite pieces and bake until they achieve a cooked, slightly crispy texture. These miniature liver treats are irresistible and apt for training incentives.
- ✓ **Cheese and Bacon Balls:** The allure of cheese and bacon is unparalleled for most dogs. Combine shredded cheese with finely chopped cooked bacon and whole wheat flour to shape a dough. Fashion the dough into diminutive balls and bake until they assume a golden hue. These savory morsels captivate attention during training endeavors.
- ✓ **Peanut Butter Drops:** Peanut butter stands as a beloved treat for countless canines, serving as a delectable reward in training sessions. Dispense small dollops of peanut butter onto a parchment-lined baking sheet and freeze until solid. These frozen peanut butter drops deliver a refreshing and gratifying reprieve for your pup.
- ✓ **Tuna and Carrot Squares:** Tuna, rich in protein, holds an irresistible appeal for dogs. Combine canned tuna with grated carrots and a touch of oat flour for cohesion. Press the mixture into a baking dish and bake until firm. Once cooled, slice into petite squares for a nutritious training treat.
- ✓ **Turkey and Sweet Potato Strips:** Turkey and sweet potato offer wholesome indulgence for dogs. Slice cooked turkey breast and sweet potato into slender strips and bake until they acquire a crispy consistency. These chewy strips offer a gratifying reward for your pup's commendable conduct during training.

By embracing homemade training treats, you guarantee your dog receives premium rewards devoid of additives and preservatives. These tantalizing snacks foster your pup's motivation and engagement during training sessions, facilitating their growth into well-mannered companions.

High-Value Motivators

In dog training, certain behaviors demand extra encouragement, especially in challenging settings or when imparting complex commands. High-value motivators, such as treats with significant appeal to dogs, are often employed to reinforce desired behaviors or during intensive training sessions. Typically reserved for special occasions or tasks demanding heightened focus and engagement, these treats play a pivotal role in training success. Here are some homemade high-value motivators certain to captivate your pup's attention:

- ✓ **Beef Liver Delights:** Beef liver, rich in protein and boasting a potent aroma, is irresistible to many dogs. Slice raw beef liver into thin strips and bake until they achieve a crispy texture. These crunchy delights burst with flavor, serving as excellent high-value treats for training endeavors.
- ✓ **Salmon and Spinach Bites:** Salmon, brimming with omega-3 fatty acids beneficial for skin and coat health, is both delicious and nutritious. Combine canned salmon with finely chopped spinach and oat flour to create a dough. Roll into small balls and bake until golden brown. These savory bites reward your dog's diligence during training sessions.
- ✓ **Turkey and Cheese Roll-Ups:** Turkey and cheese hold immense appeal for dogs. Spread slices of cooked turkey breast with cream cheese, roll them up, and cut into bite-sized pieces. These delectable roll-ups motivate your dog to showcase their best behavior.
- ✓ **Blueberry Yogurt Drops:** Blueberries, packed with antioxidants and vitamins, contribute to your dog's overall health. Mix mashed blueberries with plain yogurt, spread onto a baking sheet, and freeze until solid. Cut into small pieces for a refreshing and nutritious high-value treat option.
- ✓ **Chicken and Pumpkin Meatballs:** Chicken and pumpkin offer a bounty of nutrients. Combine shredded cooked chicken with mashed pumpkin and rolled oats, forming small meatballs. Bake until cooked through. These moist and flavorful meatballs keep your dog engaged and motivated during training.

Employing high-value motivators in your training regimen bolsters the bond between you and your dog while enhancing the effectiveness of desired behaviors. These homemade treats offer a healthy and delectable alternative to store-bought options, ensuring your furry friend receives only the finest rewards for their efforts.

Small Bites for Frequent Rewards

When it comes to training your furry companion, frequent rewards are essential for reinforcing positive behaviors and maintaining engagement. Small, bite-sized treats are ideal for this purpose, as they can be dispensed quickly and won't fill up your dog too quickly during training sessions. Here are some simple and nutritious homemade recipes for small bites that are perfect for frequent rewards:

Chicken and Sweet Potato Squares:

Ingredients:

- 1 cup cooked chicken breast, diced
- 1/2 cup mashed sweet potato
- 1 egg
- 1/4 cup oat flour

Instructions:

- Preheat the oven to 350°F (175°C) and line a baking sheet with parchment paper.
- In a bowl, combine the diced chicken breast, mashed sweet potato, egg, and oat flour until well mixed.
- Spread the mixture onto the prepared baking sheet and smooth it out evenly.
- Bake for 20-25 minutes until firm and lightly browned.
- Allow to cool, then cut into small squares.

Nutritional Values (per serving):

- Protein: 6g
- Fat: 3g
- Carbohydrates: 8g

Peanut Butter and Banana Balls:

Ingredients:
- 1 ripe banana, mashed
- 1/4 cup natural peanut butter
- 1 cup rolled oats

Instructions:
- In a bowl, combine the mashed banana and peanut butter until smooth.
- Stir in the rolled oats until well incorporated.
- Roll the mixture into small balls and place them on a baking sheet lined with parchment paper.
- Flatten each ball slightly with a fork.
- Bake at 325°F (160°C) for 10-12 minutes until lightly golden.

Nutritional Values (per serving):
- Protein: 3g
- Fat: 5g
- Carbohydrates: 10g

Cheesy Oatmeal Bites:

Ingredients:

- 1 cup cooked oatmeal
- 1/2 cup shredded cheddar cheese
- 1 egg

Instructions:

- Preheat the oven to 350°F (175°C) and grease a mini muffin tin.
- In a bowl, mix the cooked oatmeal, shredded cheddar cheese, and egg until combined.
- Spoon the mixture into the mini muffin tin, filling each cavity halfway.
- Bake for 12-15 minutes until set and golden brown.
- Allow to cool before serving.

Nutritional Values (per serving):

- Protein: 4g
- Fat: 6g
- Carbohydrates: 8g

These small bites are not only delicious but also provide essential nutrients to support your dog's overall health and well-being. Use them as frequent rewards during training sessions to keep your furry friend motivated and eager to learn.

Long-lasting chews for Extended Engagement

Long-lasting treats are an excellent choice for dogs who enjoy a good chew and need something to occupy their time. These snacks offer mental engagement, support dental well-being, and fulfill your dog's instinctive desire to chew. Here are some homemade recipes for long-lasting chews that will keep your furry friend engaged:

Sweet Potato Chews:

Ingredients:

- ✓ 2 large sweet potatoes

Instructions:

- ✓ Preheat the oven to 250°F (120°C) and line a baking sheet with parchment paper.
- ✓ Wash the sweet potatoes and slice them lengthwise into thin strips, about 1/4 inch thick.
- ✓ Place the sweet potato slices on the prepared baking sheet in a single layer.
- ✓ Bake for 3-4 hours until the slices are dried and slightly chewy.
- ✓ Let them cool completely before giving them to your dog.

Nutritional Values (per serving):

- ✓ Fiber: 3g
- ✓ Vitamin A: 400% DV
- ✓ Vitamin C: 4% DV

Frozen Carrot Sticks:

Ingredients:

- ✓ Carrots, washed and peeled

Instructions:

- ✓ Cut the carrots into long sticks, similar to the size of commercial dog chews.
- ✓ Place the carrot sticks on a baking sheet lined with parchment paper.
- ✓ Freeze them for at least 2 hours until they are firm.
- ✓ Once frozen, store them in a resealable bag in the freezer until ready to use.

Nutritional Values (per serving):

- ✓ Fiber: 2g
- ✓ Vitamin A: 184% DV
- ✓ Vitamin K: 14% DV

Peanut Butter Stuffed Kong:

Ingredients:

- 1 Kong toy
- Natural peanut butter

Instructions:

- Fill the Kong toy with natural peanut butter, leaving some space at the top.
- Place the filled Kong in the freezer for a few hours until the peanut butter hardens.
- Give the frozen Kong to your dog as a long-lasting chew and mental stimulation toy.

Nutritional Values (per serving):

- Protein: 8g
- Fat: 16g
- Carbohydrates: 8g

These long-lasting chews are not only enjoyable for your dog but also beneficial for their dental health and overall well-being. Incorporate them into your dog's routine to provide hours of entertainment and satisfaction.

Chapter 6:
Seasonal and Celebration Treats

Seasonal and celebration treats for dogs present a delightful opportunity to pamper your furry friend while infusing a festive spirit into their routine. Much like humans, dogs relish special indulgences during holidays and seasonal festivities. These treats also offer a chance to introduce seasonal ingredients into your dog's diet, diversifying their nutrition while adding a touch of flair.

During holidays such as Christmas, Easter, Halloween, or your dog's birthday, homemade treats can become a cherished part of the celebration. Crafting festive-shaped treats using cookie cutters or molds adorned with dog-friendly icing or yogurt adds charm to the occasion. These treats not only exude cuteness but can also be customized to cater to your dog's palate and dietary requirements.

Seasonal ingredients like pumpkin, cranberries, and apples lend themselves well to treats for fall or Thanksgiving-themed revelries. Pumpkin, in particular, boasts high nutritional value for dogs, offering fiber and essential vitamins. Incorporate it into pumpkin cookies, muffins, or frozen pumpkin treats for a flavorful twist.

In summer, frozen treats emerge as a refreshing and enjoyable way to beat the heat. Whip up frozen yogurt bites using plain yogurt and fresh fruits like blueberries or strawberries. Simply blend the ingredients, pour the mixture into ice cube trays or silicone molds, and freeze until solid. These treats not only tantalize the taste buds but also provide hydration and nourishment.

Marking your dog's birthday or gotcha day with a bespoke homemade cake or pup cakes can create enduring memories of affection and celebration. Numerous dog-friendly cake recipes feature ingredients like peanut butter, banana, and whole wheat flour. However, exercise caution to avoid ingredients potentially harmful to dogs, such as chocolate, xylitol, or excessive sugar.

In essence, seasonal and celebration treats infuse joy and anticipation into your dog's routine, fostering a deeper bond through the shared experience of baking and savoring delicious treats. By employing simple, wholesome ingredients and remaining mindful of your dog's dietary considerations, you can concoct homemade delights that are both safe and delightful for your loyal companion.

Festive Holiday Snacks

Festive holiday snacks for dogs are a delightful way to include your furry friend in seasonal celebrations. These treats allow you to share the joy of special occasions with your canine companion while ensuring they stay healthy and happy. Here are some delicious and nutritious holiday snacks that your dog will love:

Christmas Turkey Bites:

Ingredients:

- ✓ Cooked turkey breast
- ✓ Sweet potatoes
- ✓ Whole wheat flour
- ✓ Eggs.

Nutritional Values:

- ✓ Protein: 8g
- ✓ Fat: 3g
- ✓ Carbohydrates: 12g (per serving).

Instructions:

- ✓ Dice-cooked turkey breast and mashed sweet potatoes.
- ✓ Mix with whole wheat flour and eggs until a dough forms.
- ✓ Roll out the dough and cut into small shapes.
- ✓ Bake until golden brown.

Easter Carrot Pup cakes:

Ingredients:
- ✓ Carrots
- ✓ Oats
- ✓ Unsweetened applesauce
- ✓ Honey
- ✓ Baking powder

Nutritional Values:
- ✓ Protein: 4g
- ✓ Fat: 2g
- ✓ Carbohydrates: 8g (per pup cake).

Instructions:
- ✓ Grate carrots and mix with oats, applesauce, honey, and baking powder.
- ✓ Pour into cupcake molds and bake until set.
- ✓ Decorate with a dollop of yogurt.

Halloween Pumpkin Treats:

Ingredients:

- ✓ Pumpkin puree
- ✓ Oat flour
- ✓ Cinnamon
- ✓ Eggs.

Nutritional Values:

- ✓ Protein: 3g
- ✓ Fat: 1g
- ✓ Carbohydrates: 6g (per serving).

Instructions:

- ✓ Combine pumpkin puree, oat flour, cinnamon, and eggs until well combined.
- ✓ Form into small balls and flatten them with a fork.
- ✓ Bake until firm.

Thanksgiving Cranberry Cookies:

Ingredients:
- ✓ Dried cranberries
- ✓ Almond flour
- ✓ Eggs
- ✓ Coconut oil

Nutritional Values:
- ✓ Protein: 2g
- ✓ Fat: 4g
- ✓ Carbohydrates: 5g (per cookie).

Instructions:
- ✓ Mix dried cranberries, almond flour, eggs, and melted coconut oil.
- ✓ Roll out the dough and cut it into cookie shapes.
- ✓ Bake until lightly golden.

Valentine's Day Berry Hearts:

Ingredients:

- ✓ Strawberries
- ✓ Blueberries
- ✓ Plain yogurt
- ✓ Honey.

Nutritional Values:

- ✓ Protein: 1g
- ✓ Fat: 0.5g
- ✓ Carbohydrates: 3g (per heart).

Instructions:

- ✓ Blend strawberries, blueberries, yogurt, and honey until smooth.
- ✓ Pour into heart-shaped molds and freeze until solid.

These festive holiday snacks are not only tasty but also packed with nutrients to keep your dog healthy and satisfied. Remember to adjust the portion sizes according to your dog's size and dietary requirements. With these homemade treats, your dog can join in the holiday fun while enjoying delicious and wholesome snacks made with love.

Birthday and Party Treats

Planning a special celebration for your furry friend's birthday or a doggy party? Make it even more memorable with homemade treats tailored for the occasion. These birthday and party treats are not only delicious but also healthy, ensuring your dog enjoys every moment without any guilt. Here are some delightful recipes to mark the occasion:

Peanut Butter Pup cakes:

Ingredients:
- Whole wheat flour
- Baking powder
- Peanut butter
- Applesauce
- Eggs.

Nutritional Values:
- Protein: 5g
- Fat: 3g
- Carbohydrates: 10g (per pup cake).

Instructions:
- Mix whole wheat flour and baking powder, then add peanut butter, applesauce, and eggs.
- Pour into cupcake molds and bake until golden brown.

Cheesy Bone Biscuits:

Ingredients:
- ✓ Rolled oats
- ✓ Grated cheese
- ✓ Chicken broth
- ✓ Egg.

Nutritional Values:
- ✓ Protein: 6g
- ✓ Fat: 4g
- ✓ Carbohydrates: 8g (per biscuit).

Instructions:
- ✓ Combine rolled oats, grated cheese, and chicken broth.
- ✓ Add egg to bind the mixture. Roll out and cut into bone shapes.
- ✓ Bake until crispy.

Apple and Carrot Paws:

Ingredients:
- ✓ Whole wheat flour
- ✓ Grated apple
- ✓ Grated carrot
- ✓ Honey
- ✓ Egg.

Nutritional Values: P
- ✓ Protein: 3g
- ✓ Fat: 2g
- ✓ Carbohydrates: 6g (per paw).

Instructions:
- ✓ Mix whole wheat flour, grated apple, grated carrot, honey, and egg.
- ✓ Shape into paw prints and bake until firm.

Blueberry Banana Bites:

Ingredients:
- Oat flour
- Mashed banana
- Blueberries
- Yogurt.

Nutritional Values:
- Protein: 2g
- Fat: 1.5g
- Carbohydrates: 4g (per bite).

Instructions:
- Combine oat flour, mashed banana, and blueberries.
- Form into small balls and freeze.
- Dip in yogurt before serving.

Salmon and Sweet Potato Stars:

Ingredients:

- Cooked salmon
- Mashed sweet potato
- Oat flour
- Egg.

Nutritional Values:

- Protein: 7g
- Fat: 4g
- Carbohydrates: 9g (per star).

Instructions:

- Mix cooked salmon, mashed sweet potato, oat flour, and egg.
- Roll out and cut into star shapes.
- Bake until golden.

These birthday and party treats will make your dog feel extra special on their big day or during any festive gathering. Remember to adjust the portion sizes based on your dog's size and dietary needs. With these homemade delights, your pup's celebration is sure to be a hit!

Cooling Summer Snacks

When the weather heats up, it's essential to keep your canine companion cool and refreshed. These cooling summer snacks will not only help beat the heat but also provide a tasty treat for your furry friend. Let's dive into some easy and refreshing recipes:

Frozen Yogurt Drops:

Ingredients:

- Plain yogurt
- Mashed banana
- Honey.

Nutritional Values:

- Protein: 2g
- Fat: 1g
- Carbohydrates: 3g (per drop).

Instructions:

- Mix plain yogurt with mashed banana and honey.
- Drop a small spoonful onto a baking sheet and freeze until solid.

Watermelon Ice Cubes:

Ingredients:

- ✓ Watermelon
- ✓ Water.

Nutritional Values:

- ✓ Protein: 0.6g
- ✓ Fat: 0.2g
- ✓ Carbohydrates: 9g (per cube).

Instructions:

- ✓ Puree watermelon and mix it with water.
- ✓ Pour into ice cube trays and freeze.
- ✓ Serve as a refreshing snack.

Cucumber Mint Bites:

Ingredients:
- Cucumber
- Fresh mint leaves
- Water.

Nutritional Values:
- Protein: 0.4g
- Fat: 0.1g
- Carbohydrates: 1.5g (per bite).

Instructions:
- Blend cucumber and mint leaves with water.
- Pour into molds and freeze until solid.

Coconut Water Popsicles:

Ingredients:
- Coconut water
- Diced strawberries
- Diced kiwi.

Nutritional Values:
- Protein: 0.5g
- Fat: 0.2g
- Carbohydrates: 4g (per popsicle).

Instructions:
- Mix coconut water with diced strawberries and kiwi.
- Pour into popsicle molds and freeze.

Frozen Blueberry Bites:

Ingredients:

- ✓ Blueberries
- ✓ Plain yogurt.

Nutritional Values:

- ✓ Protein: 1g
- ✓ Fat: 0.5g
- ✓ Carbohydrates: 4g (per bite).

Instructions:

- ✓ Dip blueberries in plain yogurt and freeze on a baking sheet.
- ✓ Serve once frozen.

These cooling summer snacks are not only hydrating but also packed with nutrients to keep your dog healthy and happy during the hot months. Remember to supervise your pet while enjoying these treats, especially with frozen options, to prevent choking hazards. With these simple and refreshing recipes, your furry friend will stay cool and satisfied all summer long.

Chapter 7: Advanced Nutritious Recipes

Crafting advanced nutritious recipes for your four-legged companion can significantly enhance their diet, ensuring they receive essential nutrients for optimal health. These recipes surpass basic treats, offering a diverse array of flavors and textures to keep your dog both excited and fulfilled. Let's delve into the significance of incorporating advanced nutritious recipes into your dog's culinary repertoire:

- ✓ **Enhanced Nutritional Value:** Advanced recipes encompass a broader spectrum of ingredients, allowing you to customize your dog's treats to meet their specific nutritional requirements. By incorporating ingredients rich in vitamins, minerals, and antioxidants, you can bolster your dog's overall well-being and bolster their immune system.
- ✓ **Variety and Interest:** Just like humans, dogs relish diversity in their meals. Advanced recipes introduce a medley of flavors and textures, warding off monotony and enticing your dog to relish their treats. Experimenting with a variety of ingredients can also help discerning eaters discover new favorites.
- ✓ **Joint and Bone Health:** Certain advanced recipes may integrate ingredients like glucosamine and chondroitin, renowned for their role in supporting joint health and mobility. These treats prove particularly beneficial for senior dogs or breeds predisposed to joint concerns.
- ✓ **Digestive Health:** Ingredients such as probiotics and fiber play a pivotal role in promoting healthy digestion among dogs. Advanced recipes may incorporate elements like pumpkin, sweet potatoes, or yogurt, renowned for their gentleness on the digestive system and ability to regulate bowel movements.
- ✓ **Weight Management:** For dogs necessitating weight management, advanced recipes can be tailored to encompass low-calorie ingredients without compromising on flavor and satisfaction. By integrating lean proteins, vegetables, and fruits, you can help your dog feel satiated while effectively managing their weight.
- ✓ **Allergy Management:** In instances where your dog grapples with food sensitivities or allergies, advanced recipes enable you to meticulously select

ingredients that align with their dietary needs. Steering clear of common allergens such as wheat, soy, and dairy can mitigate the risk of adverse reactions.

By integrating advanced nutritious recipes into your dog's culinary repertoire, you furnish them with an extensive array of nutrients while ensuring their meals remain captivating and enjoyable. Whether you seek to bolster their joint health, enhance digestion, or manage their weight, a plethora of nutritious ingredients and recipes await exploration. Remember to seek guidance from your veterinarian before effecting any significant alterations to your dog's diet, especially if they harbor specific health concerns or dietary constraints.

Superfood Snacks

Indulging our beloved pets with nutritious treats is a joyous endeavor, and integrating superfoods into their snacks can provide a significant boost of essential nutrients, vitamins, and antioxidants. These superfood-infused treats not only tantalize your dog's taste buds but also contribute to their overall health and well-being.

Superfoods are revered for their nutrient-rich profiles and health-enhancing properties. By incorporating them into homemade dog treats, you can offer your furry companion an array of benefits. Here are some commonly used superfoods in dog treats:

- ✓ **Blueberries:** Bursting with antioxidants and vitamins C and K, blueberries support immune function and cognitive health in dogs.
- ✓ **Spinach:** Abundant in iron, vitamins A, C, and K, and fiber, spinach aids digestion and fortifies bone health.
- ✓ **Pumpkin:** Rich in fiber and beta-carotene, pumpkin aids digestion and fosters a lustrous coat.
- ✓ **Sweet Potatoes:** Packed with vitamins A and C and fiber, sweet potatoes support digestion and help regulate blood sugar levels.
- ✓ **Salmon:** Rich in omega-3 fatty acids, salmon promotes skin and coat health, reduces inflammation, and bolsters heart health.
- ✓ **Coconut Oil:** Renowned for its antibacterial and antifungal properties, coconut oil enhances skin health and aids digestion.
- ✓ **Chia Seeds:** Brimming with omega-3 fatty acids, fiber, and protein, chia seeds bolster digestion and supply a burst of energy.
- ✓ **Turmeric:** With its anti-inflammatory properties, turmeric alleviates joint pain and boosts overall immune function.

When concocting superfood snacks for your furry friend, consider synergizing these ingredients to amplify their nutritional potency. For instance, you might whip up blueberry and spinach muffins or craft pumpkin and sweet potato biscuits. Utilize fresh, top-quality ingredients, and steer clear of artificial flavors, colors, or preservatives.

To ensure your dog reaps the full nutritional benefits from these superfood snacks, adhere to precise ingredient quantities in your recipes. This preserves the integrity of the recipe and facilitates achieving the desired nutritional balance for your four-legged friend.

Before introducing any new treats into your dog's diet, seek advice from your veterinarian, particularly if your pet has specific dietary needs or health concerns. Armed with the right combination of superfoods, you can delight your furry companion with delectable and nourishing snacks that bolster their overall health and happiness.

Homemade Meals and Meal Toppers

Crafting homemade meals and meal toppers presents a remarkable opportunity to ensure your beloved pet enjoys a diet brimming with nutrition and balance. By preparing your dog's food at home, you wield control over the ingredients, enabling customization to suit their specific dietary requirements and preferences. Moreover, meal toppers infuse variety and excitement into your dog's dining experience, captivating even the most discerning of palates.

When venturing into the realm of homemade meals for your canine companion, it's imperative to strike a harmonious balance of protein, carbohydrates, healthy fats, vitamins, and minerals. Here are some nutrient-rich ingredients commonly featured in homemade dog meals and meal toppers:

- ✓ **Proteins:** Opt for lean meats such as chicken, turkey, beef, or fish, which furnish essential amino acids crucial for muscle growth and repair.
- ✓ **Carbohydrates:** Whole grains like brown rice, quinoa, or oats serve as wholesome sources of carbohydrates, furnishing energy and fiber for digestive health. Additionally, vegetables such as sweet potatoes, carrots, and green beans provide 99carbohydrates alongside a bounty of vitamins and minerals.
- ✓ **Healthy Fats:** Integrate nourishing fats such as salmon oil, flaxseed oil, or coconut oil into your dog's meals to bolster skin and coat health, cognitive function, and overall vitality.
- ✓ **Fruits and Vegetables:** Elevate your dog's meals with nutrient-rich fruits like blueberries, apples, and bananas, as well as vegetables such as spinach, broccoli,

and peas, which supply vital vitamins, minerals, and antioxidants. These ingredients not only enhance flavor and texture but also amplify nutritional value.

To concoct a homemade meal tailored to your dog's needs, simply amalgamate cooked protein, carbohydrates, healthy fats, and an array of fruits and vegetables in suitable proportions. Ensure thorough cooking to guarantee safety and allow the meal to cool before serving.

For meal toppers, merely chop or puree ingredients like cooked meat, vegetables, or fruits, and sprinkle them over your dog's regular kibble to enhance its flavor and nutritional profile.

When gauging portion sizes for homemade meals and meal toppers, factor in your dog's size, age, activity level, and any dietary restrictions or health concerns they may harbor. Maintaining a well-rounded diet is imperative to stave off nutrient deficiencies or surpluses.

By incorporating homemade meals and toppers into your dog's culinary repertoire, you furnish them with nourishing sustenance and delectable flavors they'll relish. Delve into experimentation with diverse ingredients and recipes to unearth the ideal amalgamation for your furry friend's discerning palate and nutritional requisites.

Therapeutic Treats for Health Issues

Therapeutic treats for dogs can be a wonderful addition to their diet, offering targeted nutritional support for various health issues. These treats are carefully crafted to address specific concerns and can aid in managing conditions such as joint pain, digestive problems, anxiety, and skin issues. When creating therapeutic treats for your furry friend, it's crucial to choose ingredients known for their beneficial properties and to follow precise recipes to ensure effectiveness.

- ✓ **Joint Health Treats:** For dogs experiencing joint pain or stiffness, treats containing glucosamine, chondroitin, and omega-3 fatty acids can provide relief. Ingredients like salmon, sweet potatoes, and turmeric are known for their anti-inflammatory properties and can support joint health.
- ✓ **Digestive Support Treats:** Treats formulated to aid digestion often include ingredients like pumpkin, yogurt, and probiotics. These ingredients promote a healthy balance of gut bacteria and can alleviate symptoms of digestive upset such as diarrhea or constipation.

- ✓ **Anxiety Relief Treats:** Dogs suffering from anxiety may benefit from treats containing calming ingredients like chamomile, valerian root, or CBD oil. These ingredients can help soothe nervousness and promote relaxation without causing drowsiness.
- ✓ **Skin and Coat Health Treats:** Treats designed to improve skin and coat health typically contain ingredients rich in omega-3 and omega-6 fatty acids, such as fish oil, flaxseed, and coconut oil. These fatty acids support a shiny coat and healthy skin, reducing itching and irritation.

When preparing therapeutic treats for your dog, it's essential to follow recipes closely to ensure proper dosing and effectiveness. Here's an example recipe for joint health treats:

Ingredients:
- ✓ 1 cup cooked salmon, shredded
- ✓ 1/2 cup cooked sweet potato, mashed
- ✓ 1 tablespoon ground turmeric
- ✓ 1 tablespoon glucosamine powder
- ✓ 1 tablespoon chia seeds

Instructions:
- ✓ Preheat the oven to 350°F (175°C) and line a baking sheet with parchment paper.
- ✓ In a mixing bowl, combine the shredded salmon, mashed sweet potato, turmeric, glucosamine powder, and chia seeds. Mix until well combined.
- ✓ Roll the mixture into small balls or flatten into shapes using your hands.
- ✓ Place the treats onto the prepared baking sheet and bake for 15-20 minutes or until firm and golden brown.
- ✓ Allow the treats to cool completely before serving to your dog.

By incorporating therapeutic treats into your dog's diet, you can provide targeted support for their specific health needs while offering them a delicious and nutritious snack. Always consult your veterinarian before introducing new treats or supplements, especially if your dog has underlying health conditions or is taking medication.

Chapter 8: Storing and Preserving Your Homemade Treats

Effectively storing and preserving homemade dog treats is crucial to uphold their freshness and nutritional value. Implementing proper storage techniques not only prevents spoilage but also extends the shelf life of the treats, ensuring your furry friend can relish them safely for an extended period. Here are some practical tips for storing and preserving homemade dog treats:

- ✓ **Allow Cooling Time:** Ensure homemade treats cool completely before storage. Warm treats placed in containers can foster condensation, potentially leading to moisture accumulation and mold formation.
- ✓ **Opt for Air-Tight Containers:** Store homemade treats in air-tight containers to shield them from air exposure, moisture, and pests. Glass jars with sealed lids or tight-fitting plastic containers are excellent choices for preserving treats.
- ✓ **Refrigerate Perishables:** If homemade treats contain perishable ingredients like meat, cheese, or yogurt, refrigerate them to prolong freshness. Refrigeration slows bacterial growth and helps maintain treatment quality.
- ✓ **Consider Freezing:** For extended storage, freezing homemade treats is an option. Place the treats in a single layer on a parchment-lined baking sheet and freeze until solid. Afterward, move them to containers or bags that are safe for the freezer. Frozen treats typically retain quality for several months.
- ✓ **Label and Date:** To track expiration dates and ingredients, label each container or bag of treats with the preparation date and treat type. This facilitates treatment rotation and ensures timely consumption before expiration.
- ✓ **Minimize Moisture Exposure:** Keep treats away from high-humidity areas like kitchen sinks or dishwashers, as moisture can cause treats to become soggy and susceptible to mold growth.
- ✓ **Regular Inspection:** Periodically examine stored treats for spoilage signs such as mold, unusual odors, or texture changes. Discard any treats showing signs of deterioration to prevent your dog from consuming spoiled food.

- ✓ **Rotate Treat Stock:** Adopt a "first in, first out" approach to treat storage to use older treats before newer ones. This prevents treats from languishing in storage and ensures your dog always accesses fresh snacks.

By adhering to these storage and preservation practices, you can uphold the quality and safety of your homemade dog treats, allowing your furry companion to savor them for extended periods while safeguarding their health and well-being.

Safe Storage Practices

Ensuring the safe storage of homemade dog treats is paramount to preserving their freshness and quality. Proper storage not only maintains the treats' safety but also safeguards their flavor and nutritional value. Here are essential guidelines for safely storing homemade dog treats:

- ✓ **Cooling Before Storage:** Before storing homemade treats, allow them to cool completely. Placing warm treats in containers can cause condensation, leading to moisture buildup and potential spoilage. Cooling treats on wire racks promotes air circulation, aiding in the cooling process.
- ✓ **Air-Tight Containers:** Store homemade treats in air-tight containers to shield them from air exposure, moisture, and pests. Opt for containers with sealable lids that fit tightly to retain freshness. Glass jars or plastic containers with secure lids are ideal for storing treats.
- ✓ **Refrigeration:** Treats containing perishable ingredients like meat, cheese, or yogurt should be refrigerated to prolong their shelf life. Refrigeration slows bacterial growth and helps maintain treatment quality. Store refrigerated treats in containers or bags to prevent cross-contamination.
- ✓ **Freezing:** Extend the shelf life of homemade treats by freezing them. Place treats in a single layer on a parchment-lined baking sheet and freeze until solid. Transfer frozen treats to freezer-safe containers or bags. Frozen treats can typically be stored for several months.
- ✓ **Labeling and Dating:** Label each container or bag of treats with the preparation date and treat type to track expiration dates and ingredients. This practice facilitates treatment rotation and ensures timely consumption before expiration. Note any special dietary considerations or allergens for easy reference.
- ✓ **Avoiding Moisture:** Keep homemade treats away from areas of high humidity, such as the kitchen sink or dishwasher, to prevent moisture buildup. Ensure

containers are tightly sealed to prevent moisture infiltration, preserving great quality.
- ✓ **Regular Inspection:** Periodically inspect stored treats for signs of spoilage, such as mold growth, unusual odors, or changes in texture. Discard any treats showing signs of deterioration to prevent your dog from consuming spoiled food.
- ✓ **Rotation:** Adopt a "first in, first out" approach when storing treats to prioritize older treats. This prevents treats from lingering in storage for too long and ensures your dog always enjoys fresh snacks.

By adhering to these safe storage practices, you can prolong the shelf life of homemade dog treats, ensuring they remain safe and delightful for your furry companion.

Freezing and Dehydrating

Freezing and dehydrating are two effective methods for preserving homemade dog treats, allowing pet owners to extend the shelf life of their creations while maintaining their nutritional value. Here's how you can utilize these methods:

Freezing:

Freezing homemade dog treats is a convenient way to store them for an extended period without compromising their quality. This method works well for treats that contain ingredients like meat, cheese, or yogurt.

- ✓ **Preparation:** After baking or preparing the treats, allow them to cool completely to room temperature.
- ✓ **Packaging:** Place the cooled treats in a single layer on a baking sheet lined with parchment paper. This prevents them from sticking together during freezing.
- ✓ **Freezing:** Transfer the baking sheet to the freezer and let the treats freeze until they are solid. This usually takes a few hours.
- ✓ **Storage:** Once frozen, transfer the treats to airtight containers or resealable freezer bags. Label the containers with the date of freezing and the type of treats inside for easy identification.
- ✓ **Usage:** Frozen treats can be stored in the freezer for several months. When needed, simply remove the desired quantity of treats from the freezer and thaw them in the refrigerator or at room temperature before serving them to your furry friend.

Dehydrating:

Dehydrating is another method for preserving homemade dog treats, especially those with a higher moisture content. This method removes moisture from the treats, making them less prone to spoilage.

- ✓ **Preparation:** Prepare the treats according to the recipe and allow them to cool completely.
- ✓ **Slicing:** For treats that are soft or chewy, slice them into uniform pieces using a sharp knife or kitchen shears. This ensures even drying.
- ✓ **Dehydrator Setup:** Arrange the treats in a single layer on the trays of a food dehydrator, leaving space between each piece for air circulation.
- ✓ **Dehydrating:** Set the dehydrator to the appropriate temperature and drying time according to the manufacturer's instructions. Treats typically need to be dried at low temperatures (around 130°F to 160°F) for several hours until they are firm and dry to the touch.
- ✓ **Cooling and Storage:** Allow the dehydrated treats to cool completely before storing them in airtight containers or resealable bags. Label the containers with the date and type of treats.

Both freezing and dehydrating are excellent methods for preserving homemade dog treats, allowing pet owners to provide their furry companions with nutritious and delicious snacks for longer periods. By following these methods, you can ensure that your homemade treats remain fresh, flavorful, and safe for your dog to enjoy.

Best Before: Understanding Shelf Life

Understanding the shelf life of homemade dog treats is crucial for ensuring their freshness, safety, and nutritional value. While these treats don't contain preservatives like store-bought options, proper storage and handling practices can help prolong their shelf life. Here's what you need to know:

- ✓ **Ingredients Matter:** The shelf life of homemade dog treats largely depends on the ingredients used. Treats made with perishable ingredients like meat, cheese, or fresh vegetables will have a shorter shelf life compared to treats made with dry ingredients like oats or flour.
- ✓ **Storage Conditions:** Proper storage is key to extending the shelf life of homemade dog treats. Store treats in airtight containers or resealable bags to protect them from moisture, air, and pests. Keep them in a cool, dry place away from direct sunlight, which can cause them to spoil faster.

- ✓ **Refrigeration:** Treats containing perishable ingredients should be refrigerated to prevent bacterial growth and spoilage. While refrigeration can extend the shelf life of these treats, they should still be consumed within a few days to a week for optimal freshness.
- ✓ **Freezing:** For longer-term storage, consider freezing homemade dog treats. Treats can be frozen in airtight containers or resealable bags for several months. When needed, simply thaw them in the refrigerator or at room temperature before serving.
- ✓ **Observing Changes:** Keep an eye out for any changes in appearance, texture, or odor, as these can indicate spoilage. Discard any treats that show signs of mold, discoloration, or an off smell.
- ✓ **Nutritional Degradation:** Over time, the nutritional value of homemade dog treats may degrade, particularly if they contain ingredients that are sensitive to oxidation, such as fats and oils. To maintain their nutritional quality, it's best to consume treats within a reasonable time frame.
- ✓ **Labeling:** Properly label homemade treats with the date they were made and the type of treats inside. This makes it easier to track their shelf life and ensure that older treats are used first.

By understanding the factors that influence the shelf life of homemade dog treats and following proper storage practices, pet owners can enjoy making nutritious and delicious treats for their furry companions without worry. Regularly rotating treats and observing any changes can help ensure that dogs receive safe and wholesome snacks every time.

Shopping list of all ingredients used in the recipes.

Peanut Butter Pupcakes:

- ✓ Whole wheat flour
- ✓ Baking powder
- ✓ Peanut butter (unsalted)
- ✓ Unsweetened applesauce
- ✓ Water
- ✓ Egg

Carrot and Oat Dog Biscuits:

- ✓ Rolled oats
- ✓ Carrots
- ✓ Unsweetened applesauce
- ✓ Egg

Cheesy Sweet Potato Chews:

- ✓ Sweet potato
- ✓ Shredded cheddar cheese (unsalted)

Banana and Blueberry Frozen Treats:

- ✓ Ripe banana
- ✓ Fresh blueberries
- ✓ Plain yogurt (unsweetened)

Chicken and Brown Rice Balls:

- ✓ Cooked brown rice
- ✓ Cooked chicken
- ✓ Chicken broth (unsalted)

Pumpkin and Cinnamon Cookies:

- ✓ Canned pumpkin (unsweetened)
- ✓ Whole wheat flour
- ✓ Ground cinnamon

Salmon and Sweet Potato Sticks:

- ✓ Cooked salmon
- ✓ Sweet potato
- ✓ Oat flour

Spinach and Cheese Bites:

- ✓ Cooked spinach
- ✓ Shredded mozzarella cheese (unsalted)
- ✓ Oat flour

Turkey and Cranberry Jerky:

- ✓ Cooked turkey breast
- ✓ Dried cranberries (unsweetened)

Apple and Cheddar Pupcakes:

- ✓ Grated apple
- ✓ Shredded cheddar cheese (unsalted)
- ✓ Unsweetened applesauce
- ✓ Water
- ✓ Egg

Beef and Potato Bites:

- ✓ Cooked beef
- ✓ Mashed potato
- ✓ Oat flour

Cranberry and Pumpkin Doggy Donuts:

- ✓ Canned pumpkin (unsweetened)
- ✓ Dried cranberries (unsweetened)
- ✓ Oat flour

Turkey Bacon Bites:

- ✓ Cooked turkey bacon
- ✓ Oat flour
- ✓ Unsweetened applesauce

Blueberry and Banana Muffins:

- ✓ Mashed banana
- ✓ Fresh blueberries
- ✓ Unsweetened applesauce
- ✓ Egg
- ✓ Oat flour

Cheese and Bacon Twists:

- ✓ Shredded cheddar cheese (unsalted)
- ✓ Cooked bacon bits
- ✓ Oat flour
- ✓ Unsweetened applesauce

Peanut Butter and Banana Frozen Treats:

- ✓ Ripe banana
- ✓ Peanut butter
- ✓ Plain yogurt (unsweetened)

Liver and Carrot Bites:

- ✓ Cooked liver
- ✓ Grated carrot
- ✓ Oat flour
- ✓ Egg

Pumpkin and Peanut Butter Biscuits:

- ✓ Canned pumpkin (unsweetened)
- ✓ Peanut butter
- ✓ Oat flour

Turkey and Veggie Meatballs:

- ✓ Cooked turkey
- ✓ Grated zucchini
- ✓ Grated carrot
- ✓ Oat flour
- ✓ Egg

Apple and Carrot Crunchies:

- ✓ Grated apple
- ✓ Grated carrot
- ✓ Oat flour

Spinach and Salmon Bites:

- ✓ Cooked salmon
- ✓ Cooked spinach
- ✓ Oat flour
- ✓ Egg

Pumpkin and Carrot Pupcakes:

- ✓ Canned pumpkin (unsweetened)
- ✓ Grated carrot
- ✓ Unsweetened applesauce
- ✓ Water
- ✓ Egg
- ✓ Oat flour

Turkey and Rice Cookies:

- ✓ Cooked turkey
- ✓ Cooked brown rice
- ✓ Unsweetened applesauce

Sweet Potato and Banana Treats:

- ✓ Mashed sweet potato
- ✓ Ripe banana, mashed
- ✓ Unsweetened applesauce
- ✓ Oat flour

Chicken and Pumpkin Poppers:

- ✓ Cooked chicken
- ✓ Canned pumpkin (unsweetened)
- ✓ Oat flour
- ✓ Egg

Blueberry and Coconut Cookies:

- ✓ Fresh blueberries, mashed
- ✓ Shredded unsweetened coconut
- ✓ Unsweetened applesauce
- ✓ Oat flour

Liver and Oatmeal Biscuits:

- ✓ Cooked liver, finely chopped
- ✓ Unsweetened applesauce
- ✓ Oat flour

Turkey and Cranberry Poppers:

- ✓ Cooked turkey, shredded
- ✓ Dried cranberries (unsweetened)
- ✓ Oat flour
- ✓ Egg

Carrot and Peanut Butter Cookies:

- ✓ Grated carrot
- ✓ Unsweetened applesauce
- ✓ Peanut butter
- ✓ Oat flour

Banana and Peanut Butter Frozen Pops:

- ✓ Ripe banana
- ✓ Peanut butter
- ✓ Plain yogurt (unsweetened)

Apple and Cheddar Biscuits:

- ✓ Grated apple
- ✓ Shredded cheddar cheese (unsalted)
- ✓ Unsweetened applesauce
- ✓ Oat flour

Peanut Butter and Jelly Bites:

- ✓ Peanut butter
- ✓ Unsweetened applesauce
- ✓ Oat flour
- ✓ Low-sugar fruit jam

Turkey and Vegetable Patties:

- ✓ Cooked turkey, shredded
- ✓ Grated zucchini
- ✓ Grated carrot
- ✓ Oat flour
- ✓ Egg

Blueberry and Banana Pup Pops:

- ✓ Ripe banana
- ✓ Fresh blueberries
- ✓ Plain yogurt (unsweetened)
- ✓ Water

Chicken and Spinach Balls:

- ✓ Cooked chicken, shredded
- ✓ Cooked spinach, chopped
- ✓ Oat flour
- ✓ Egg

Carrot and Zucchini Chips:

- ✓ 1 large carrot
- ✓ 1 small zucchini
- ✓ Olive oil

Salmon and Sweet Potato Balls:

- ✓ Cooked salmon
- ✓ Mashed sweet potato
- ✓ Oat flour
- ✓ Egg

Banana and Carrot Biscotti:

- ✓ Ripe banana
- ✓ Grated carrot
- ✓ Unsweetened applesauce
- ✓ Oat flour

Turkey and Quinoa Balls:

- ✓ Cooked turkey
- ✓ Cooked quinoa
- ✓ Oat flour
- ✓ Egg

Pumpkin and Cinnamon Twists:

- ✓ Canned pumpkin (unsweetened)
- ✓ Ground cinnamon
- ✓ Oat flour

Cheese and Parsley Biscuits:

- ✓ Shredded cheddar cheese (unsalted)
- ✓ Fresh parsley
- ✓ Unsweetened applesauce
- ✓ Oat flour

Pumpkin and Peanut Butter Bites:

- ✓ Canned pumpkin (unsweetened)
- ✓ Peanut butter
- ✓ Unsweetened applesauce
- ✓ Oat flour

Chicken and Carrot Cookies:

- ✓ Cooked chicken
- ✓ Grated carrot
- ✓ Unsweetened applesauce
- ✓ Oat flour

Blueberry and Banana Twists:

- ✓ Ripe banana
- ✓ Fresh blueberries
- ✓ Unsweetened applesauce
- ✓ Oat flour

Turkey and Cranberry Cookies:

- ✓ Cooked turkey
- ✓ Dried cranberries (unsweetened)
- ✓ Unsweetened applesauce
- ✓ Oat flour

Spinach and Feta Bites:

- ✓ Cooked spinach
- ✓ Crumbled feta cheese (unsalted)
- ✓ Unsweetened applesauce
- ✓ Oat flour

Carrot and Apple Chips:

- ✓ 1 large carrot
- ✓ 1 apple
- ✓ Olive oil

Turkey and Sweet Potato Muffins:

- ✓ Cooked turkey
- ✓ Mashed sweet potato
- ✓ Unsweetened applesauce
- ✓ Water
- ✓ Egg
- ✓ Oat flour

Chicken and Cheese Balls:

- ✓ Cooked chicken
- ✓ Shredded cheddar cheese (unsalted)
- ✓ Unsweetened applesauce
- ✓ Oat flour

Blueberry and Carrot Muffins:

- ✓ Fresh blueberries
- ✓ Grated carrot
- ✓ Unsweetened applesauce
- ✓ Water
- ✓ Egg
- ✓ Oat flour

Chicken and Sweet Potato Squares:

- ✓ Cooked chicken breast
- ✓ Mashed sweet potato
- ✓ Egg
- ✓ Oat flour

Peanut Butter and Banana Balls:

- ✓ Ripe banana
- ✓ Natural peanut butter
- ✓ Rolled oats

Cheesy Oatmeal Bites:

- ✓ Cooked oatmeal
- ✓ Shredded cheddar cheese
- ✓ Egg

Sweet Potato Chews:

- ✓ Sweet potatoes

Frozen Carrot Sticks:

- ✓ Carrots

Peanut Butter Stuffed Kong:

- ✓ Kong toy
- ✓ Natural peanut butter

Christmas Turkey Bites:

- ✓ Cooked turkey breast
- ✓ Sweet potatoes
- ✓ Whole wheat flour
- ✓ Eggs

Easter Carrot Pup cakes:

- ✓ Carrots
- ✓ Oats
- ✓ Unsweetened applesauce
- ✓ Honey
- ✓ Baking powder

Halloween Pumpkin Treats:

- ✓ Pumpkin puree
- ✓ Oat flour
- ✓ Cinnamon
- ✓ Eggs

Thanksgiving Cranberry Cookies:

- ✓ Dried cranberries
- ✓ Almond flour
- ✓ Eggs
- ✓ Coconut oil

Valentine's Day Berry Hearts:

- ✓ Strawberries
- ✓ Blueberries
- ✓ Plain yogurt
- ✓ Honey

Peanut Butter Pup cakes:

- ✓ Whole wheat flour
- ✓ Baking powder

- ✓ Peanut butter
- ✓ Applesauce
- ✓ Eggs

Cheesy Bone Biscuits:

- ✓ Rolled oats
- ✓ Grated cheese
- ✓ Chicken broth
- ✓ Egg

Apple and Carrot Paws:

- ✓ Whole wheat flour
- ✓ Grated apple
- ✓ Grated carrot
- ✓ Honey
- ✓ Egg

Blueberry Banana Bites:

- ✓ Oat flour
- ✓ Mashed banana
- ✓ Blueberries
- ✓ Yogurt

Salmon and Sweet Potato Stars:

- ✓ Cooked salmon
- ✓ Mashed sweet potato

- ✓ Oat flour
- ✓ Egg

Frozen Yogurt Drops:

- ✓ Plain yogurt
- ✓ Mashed banana
- ✓ Honey

Watermelon Ice Cubes:

- ✓ Watermelon
- ✓ Water

Cucumber Mint Bites:

- ✓ Cucumber
- ✓ Fresh mint leaves
- ✓ Water

Coconut Water Popsicles:

- ✓ Coconut water
- ✓ Diced strawberries
- ✓ Diced kiwi

Frozen Blueberry Bites:

- ✓ Blueberries
- ✓ Plain yogurt

Conclusion:

As we conclude our journey through the art of creating nutritious homemade dog treats, it's essential to reflect on the profound benefits these little labors of love bring to our furry friends. This book has equipped you with the knowledge to tailor treats to your dog's specific health needs, from managing allergies and weight to supporting joint and digestive health. Each recipe is more than just a treat; it's a gesture of your care and commitment to your dog's well-being.

By choosing to make your dog's treats, you've taken a significant step towards eliminating unnecessary additives and allergens from their diet. This proactive approach not only enhances your pet's health but also deepens the trust and bond between you. The joy seen in your dog's eager anticipation of these treats is a clear indicator of their appreciation.

We've explored various recipes, each designed to provide maximum nutritional benefits and flavor. These treats ensure that whether you are training, rewarding, or simply pampering your dog, you are contributing positively to their health. Remember, the flexibility of homemade treats allows you to adjust recipes as needed, ensuring that each treat perfectly suits your dog's taste and dietary requirements.

I encourage you to continue experimenting with ingredients and techniques as you become more confident in your treat-making skills. Share your successes and challenges with the community of like-minded dog owners, and let their experiences guide and inspire you.

Thank you for embarking on this path to creating healthier, happier lives for your dogs through the food they eat. Keep spreading the joy with every treat you bake, and remember that each small snack can make a big difference in your dog's health and happiness. Here's to many more years of joyful wagging tails and heartfelt companionship.

Reiterating the Joy and Benefits of Homemade Dog Treats

In reiterating the joy and benefits of homemade dog treats, it's essential to emphasize the profound impact they can have on your furry companion's well-being. Homemade treats offer a level of customization and control over ingredients that store-bought options often lack. By carefully selecting simple, wholesome ingredients, you can ensure that your dog's snacks are free from unnecessary additives and tailored to their specific dietary needs.

Beyond nutritional considerations, the act of preparing homemade treats fosters a deeper bond between you and your pet. Spending time in the kitchen, crafting delicious snacks can be a rewarding experience for both parties. It's an opportunity to tangibly show your love and care, all while knowing exactly what goes into the treats you're feeding your beloved pet.

Furthermore, homemade treats can contribute to your dog's overall health and happiness. By providing them with nutritious, flavorful snacks, you're helping to support their vitality and longevity. So, whether you're baking up a batch of biscuits or whipping together a special birthday treat, remember the joy and benefits that come with homemade dog treats.

Encouraging Continuous Learning and Experimentation

Encouraging continuous learning and experimentation can lead to exciting discoveries and improvements in your homemade dog treats. By staying curious and open-minded, you can explore new ingredients and techniques to enhance the nutritional value and taste of your treats. Researching different dietary requirements and preferences of dogs can also inspire you to develop recipes tailored to specific needs, such as grain-free or hypoallergenic options.

Experimentation allows you to adapt recipes based on your dog's feedback and observe their preferences. You can vary the textures, flavors, and shapes of treats to keep your furry friend engaged and excited during training sessions or as occasional rewards. Additionally, learning about different cooking methods like baking, dehydrating, or freezing can offer versatility in creating treats suitable for various occasions and seasons.

Continuous learning can not only broaden your knowledge but also strengthen your bond with your pet as you explore new ways to please them with homemade treats. Therefore, it is essential to stay curious, continue experimenting, and enjoy the process of creating healthy and delicious snacks for your beloved companion.

Building a Community of Health-Conscious Dog Owners

Creating a community of dog owners who prioritize their pet's health and well-being is an excellent way to share knowledge, experiences, and homemade treat recipes. Connecting with like-minded individuals through forums, social media groups, or local meetups can encourage responsible pet ownership and inspire homemade treat preparation.

Within this community, members can exchange ideas for healthy ingredients, discuss dietary concerns, and offer advice on creating homemade treats tailored to specific dietary needs or health issues. By sharing recipes and tips, dog owners can inspire each other to experiment with new ingredients and cooking techniques, expanding the repertoire of homemade treats available for their beloved pets.

Moreover, a community of health-conscious dog owners can serve as a valuable resource for education and support. Members can collaborate to address common challenges, such as finding suitable alternatives for dogs with food allergies or sensitivities. Together, they can navigate the journey of homemade treat preparation, ensuring that every snack is not only delicious but also nutritious and safe for their furry companions.

By fostering a sense of camaraderie and shared purpose, this community empowers dog owners to take an active role in their pets' nutrition and well-being. Through collaboration and mutual support, they can make informed choices and provide their dogs with the best possible care, one homemade treat at a time.

Recipe Development and Writing Style Notes:

As you explore the recipes and tips in this book, I encourage you to consider the following questions:

- ✓ How can you personalize the recipes to best suit your dog's preferences and dietary needs?
- ✓ What specific nutritional benefits do these recipes offer, and how can they contribute to your dog's overall health and well-being?
- ✓ How can you observe and respond to your dog's reactions to new treats, ensuring a smooth transition to any dietary changes?

Take a moment to reflect on these questions and jot down your thoughts or observations in the space provided below. Your insights and experiences will enrich your journey as a pet owner and help create a stronger bond with your furry friend.

Wishing you and your dog many happy and healthy moments together.

"As we wrap up this guide to homemade dog treats, I hope you've enjoyed your time in the kitchen, crafting healthy snacks for your beloved pet. If this book has enriched your dog's diet and brought you joy, please consider leaving a review on Amazon. Your feedback not only celebrates our shared journey but also aids in guiding fellow dog owners to make nutritious choices for their pets. It would be truly wonderful to hear your thoughts and would immensely help the dissemination of this material. Thank you for your support and happy treating!"

Printed in Great Britain
by Amazon

47416062R00071